What Relationship Experts and ...
Have to Say

"Doubling Down is an indispensable resource for anyone navigating the challenges of maintaining a dual-career household in an increasingly demanding business environment and rapidly evolving society. As a wife, a mother of two, and a business leader who has spent nearly four decades balancing the needs of my family with the demands of my career, I found the advice in this book to be highly relevant and practical for professionals at all stages of their life and career journey."

—**Marillyn Hewson**, former chairman, president and CEO, Lockheed Martin

"Buy this book if you're going to succeed as a dual-career family. Gordon and Bluestein reveal how they managed to keep love and romance alive, be great parents, and still nurture two separate careers. It's a great story, with very helpful lessons for everyone."

—**John Gottman, Ph.D.**, co-founder of The Gottman Institute and author of *The New York Times* best-seller *The Seven Principles for Making Marriage Work*

"I shared *Doubling Down* with my daughters and their husbands. Ilene and Bram truly live the principles they write about and demonstrate that, with discipline, a couple can thrive at leading a complex global company and a demanding consultancy, enjoy a loving relationship, and even raise children—yet, still find time to smile often."

—**Gregory Kenny**, Chairman of the Board of Cardinal Health and Ingredion and past president and CEO of General Cable Corporation

"The authors provide insightful and practical advice about becoming and thriving as a dual-career couple with children. Their affection for each other is very apparent and their career success is inspiring. It is all presented as a story, with helpful lessons summed up in each chapter."

—**Dianne Grande**, Ph.D., Clinical Psychologist, author of the "In It Together" blog for *Psychology Today*

"Wonderful life lessons from two amazing people who accomplished their dreams both professionally and as a family. *Doubling Down* provides real guidance on how to tackle some of life's biggest professional and personal challenges, and how successful spouses can support each other in all they do."

—**David Hanfland**, Managing Partner and Head of the Americas, Kearney

"Bram and Ilene have been one of the most committed couples: committed to their careers, to their families and to Chicago. They have always shown each other the highest respect and genuine pride in each other's accomplishments. This book reveals the secret sauce that all dual-career families can adopt to improve their own success. As a mentor to many young professionals, I am recommending they read *Doubling Down*. It is the third leg of the stool in a sustainable work-life balance world."

—**James H. Lowry**, Senior Advisor, The Boston Consulting Group, Founder of James H. Lowry & Associates and author of *Change Agent: A Life Dedicated to Creating Wealth for Minorities*

"In addition to providing real-life examples and insights into what successful dual-career couples can do to make the conflicting pieces of their lives work, this book is a wake-up call to organizations about the advantages of supporting women and men staffers who live with the sort of holistic commitment that Ilene and Bram show so consistently. *Doubling Down* is a great testament to the fact that being great at what you do doesn't require 80 hours a week, but it does require commitment, emotional intelligence and presence."

—**Tom Plath**, Senior Vice President of Human Resources, International Paper

"*Doubling Down* is part autobiography and part practical career and life advice for dual-career couples. Bram (my career coach for the past 30 years) and Ilene (an added benefit of working with Bram) have so much wisdom and guidance for dual-career couples (with and without children), which they share in this book. As a Chief People Officer, I look forward to sharing it with my organization and starting a dual-career couple resource group to help others."

—**Laura Sue D'Annunzio**, Chief People Officer, Highmetric

"In my decades studying the insights and perspectives of thousands of mothers, I have not come across a book that so insightfully articulates the creativity that successful dual-career couples need in order to bring out the best in each other. Written candidly and with humor, this guidebook to a good marriage empowers couples with children to implement creative solutions when faced with unforeseen circumstances. Even if you don't create the same rules in your household, the creativity Bram and Ilene brought to their marriage, it will inspire you to codify your own principles and game plan."

—**Michal Clements**, founder and CEO of Insight to Action and author of *Tuning into Mom: Understanding America's Most Powerful Consumer*

"*Doubling Down* contains great advice. Ilene and Bram are experienced professionals sharing a lot of knowledge about the challenges of having two careers and nourishing good family relationships. We also have faced these challenges and know that readers will be very successful if they implement many of these ideas! We have loved observing this family growing stronger every day."

—**Bonnie and Jamie Schaefer.** Bonnie is the former CEO and Co-chair of the board of Claire's Stores and Jamie is Co-owner of Westglow Resort & Spa

Doubling Down

The Secret Sauce for Dual-Career Families

Ilene Gordon and Bram Bluestein

with Kasia and Hugo Moreno

THE
BLUE SUN
PRESS

To each other, without whom this journey would never have happened!

Table of Contents

Introduction

Couples juggling two jobs are now the norm—among married-couple families with children, 64 percent have both parents employed.[1] Being part of the majority, of course, does not make it any easier to pull off. A subset of this demographic is dual-career couples, who tend to be well educated and driven by their ambitions to reach the heights of their respective professions. We are one example of such a dual-career couple.

When we met and fell in love a long time ago, we both had the same opportunity in front of us. We worked on creating a relationship of parity so that both of us could pursue our professional goals equally. It is important for couples to double down, with both wives and husbands leaning in. That's what a dual-career couple with a family is all about, which is why we are writing this book for both women and men. Businesses are now prioritizing women's leadership, and one way to boost that is by encouraging dual-career couples. While society has been making strides in recognizing women's role in business, and the traditional stereotypes of husband and wife have been adjusting to reality, women in dual-career couples still face a more uphill battle than men. That's why immediately following this introduction, we have written two separate passages from each one of us explaining what challenges we encountered because of our genders—and how we dealt with them.

Today's dual-career couples are likely to be more diversified than in the past, including gender, sexual orientation, disability status, race and ethnicity. While such couples face unique sets of challenges, we believe that much of this book will apply to almost all of them. However, since the lessons here are derived from our own experience, we haven't ventured to address various issues outside that experience. Thus, the book is written from the point of view of a heterosexual couple, but this is not intended to be exclusionary in any way.

Moreover, many situations we had to navigate, especially early in our careers, would be less common today for all sorts of reasons, whether in the workplace or social life.

We have pursued our careers, and we both achieved what we set out to do professionally. Ilene served as CEO of Ingredion and was the 21st female CEO of a Fortune 500 company. Bram had a 35-year career as a top management consultant at Booz Allen Hamilton, A.T. Kearney and the Boston Consulting Group and advised some of the largest companies in the world on addressing the most difficult and complex matters.

During the four decades of our marriage, we raised two children while both our careers were running simultaneously in high gear. To stay competitive, we had to be geographically mobile and willing to work abroad—between the two of us we accumulated more than 13 million lifetime miles from business travel (roughly 25 round trips to the moon). Neither of us stepped off our career path for any significant amount of time. We were moving forward all the time, with our foot on the accelerator. Yet we always managed to be there for our children when they needed us, and we enjoyed our Sunday night dinners together as a family. Saturday night was a date night for us as a couple. In four decades we have been apart on a Saturday maybe 10 times.

How did we manage it? We were in constant communication. There were plenty of tradeoffs. And it took resolve, grit and lots of planning, organization and creative solutions. What today you may call work-life balance hacks. Of course, when we first started working, the term "work-life balance" did not yet exist. This did not deter us. We approached our work and family life with a "we can work it out" attitude, and we were determined to be self-reliant as a family.

We did not wing it. While we weren't consciously focused on any sort of balance, we intuitively realized we had to create a thoughtful system of rules and implement certain measures to a life together. In this way, we did not waste time or risk disagreements whenever a new issue came up. We followed our agreed-upon framework, which became, in effect, our set of priorities.

One example is the 48-Hour Rule: We had to spend a full 48 hours at home on weekends before traveling again—unless we arranged a special exemption. There was flexibility built into the rule, and it assured us of two high-quality weekend days every week. Without those, we never would have made it.

In this book, we are sharing with you what has worked for us in the hope that our lessons will make it easier for you to stay on a dual-career couple track. There are so many challenging times that make the off-ramps from a dual-career track tempting. Especially after they have children, couples often negotiate career decisions and work-life balance in response to short-term pressures rather than stepping back and constructing a sustainable framework for their lives. Some of those decisions cause later regrets, whether one partner or the other gave up too much time with the children or too much lifetime earning power. We have developed a framework for persevering. It has been tested over time. It has worked for us, and we recommend it to you.

We tell our story chronologically, following the major milestones of our dual-career marriage, the challenges presented in each phase and the lessons we learned—from the first spark between us during Ilene's job interview, to changing careers and jobs and starting a family. We share with you what we believe helps with building a harmonious dual-career marriage and a balanced family.

These fundamental premises start with what kind of partners you are, where you live and what professional path you select. Our advice would be to outsource as many services as possible and split up chores based on passion, not on the basis of percentage. Also, make sure to create separate professional identities.

We also address how we have used technology to help us over the years, and how today's couples might want to think about balancing technology with "real-life" togetherness. Since we have just come out of a pandemic that has wrought havoc on dual-career couples, especially those with young children, we discuss how not to diverge from a dual-career path when the times are tough.

As such, this is a real-life playbook for a dual-career couple. We know that you don't have too much time on your hands, so we tried to make this book brief and useful, but also a fun read. The lessons are clearly marked, in case you need a fast and easy way to navigate the narrative. With every chapter, we asked ourselves this question: How will this information help a dual-career couple? We share with you very pragmatic pointers about how to create efficiencies, how to ask your bosses for more flexibility as well as the nitty-gritty of making business travel go more smoothly. We also address deeper issues such as acceptance of your spouse's success and helping your partner along their career path.

This book is for dual-career couples—and also for singles who want to become a part of such a couple—regardless of their age (from the beginning of their working life through retirement or, "rewirement"— the term was coined by Jeri Sedlar, author, senior adviser to The Conference Board on the Mature Workforce and former editor at large at *Working Woman* magazine). We believe that advice about being a dual-career couple is needed now more than ever, as the number of white-collar couples where both partners work full-time is on the rise. While among our boomer generation less than half of employees were part of dual-career couples (47 percent), that number has gone up to 78 percent among millennials.[2] Additionally, the number of couples with similar levels of education has risen by almost 25 percent over the last 30 years.[3]

We believe that succeeding as a dual-career couple requires you to be proactive with your employers to give you the flexibility and help you need to make it happen—and it worked for us 95 percent of the time. While our book is focused on enhancing dual-career couples' confidence about both partners following their professional goals, society should help more than it does. There is still plenty of bias around traditional roles defined by gender, and the expectation that men work and women stay at home has not disappeared—do not assume it has.

We believe you should each pursue your professional identity. You should also pick a city to live in that will allow each partner to develop their own career. The life you build should allow each of you to contribute to the marriage and what you are passionate about. Leave the rest to others to manage—offload any non-central duties you can.

Companies have also been slow to recognize the growing number of and the importance of dual-career couples. We believe that such couples should become recognized as an affinity group, and companies should help them achieve their goals. It is possible to think about supporting dual-career couples as a subset of women's leadership, considering that the women in such couples face more biases and responsibilities than men do. However, both women and men from dual-career couples could network together, give one another advice, support each other as a community. We hope that this book will be the start of a broader conversation about and among dual-career couples.

Please join us at our website *DoublingDownTheBook.com* to learn more about being a dual-career couple and to keep the conversation about such families going.

Ilene Gordon
Bram Bluestein

A Word From Ilene

My message to women is: Do not give up your career ambitions—they're worth it. They give you an equal seat at the table with your spouse, you contribute financially to your family, and your kids will look at you and think, "My mom is as smart as my dad." I feel that I did my part in showing society that women can be capable and that it's possible to have a career and a family.

Looking back, I am really happy I did all three things—being a professional, a spouse and a mom—at the same time. Even though society can be judgmental about mothers who decide to work full-time, and my own mother assumed that I would stop working when I had children, I was determined to have both a career and a family. One way to accomplish that was not to think about myself as being the only person good enough to be with my children, and appreciating what a great nanny, teachers and other parents can contribute.

I tried to surround myself with believers—people who accepted, and even admired, career women. A compliment from a cousin at a family party who says, "You can do it," can be empowering and push you to do more. I had no patience for any negativity.

For a dual-career couple to be balanced and happy, every professional decision of each partner needs to be viewed through the lens of what's best for the family. Women should lean in as much as men in terms of their career decision-making in the context of work and life balance. Every time you feel pressure to give up on your professional advancement or hold back, ask yourself: Would a man be expected to feel this way or make a similar decision?

Having a partner who leaned in with me, and for me, was critical. It's important to appreciate the effort that your partner is making. Men have social demands and pressures put upon them to be professionally successful and be good providers, without making any tradeoffs to jeopardize that "manly" mission. It makes me angry that society continues to stereotype us by gender. I wanted to slap every person who ever made a comment to that effect to us, but instead I just said: "It's a win-win." My answer was to pick a great spouse and insist that the rest of the world support us. In fact, I believe that a man who is married to a career woman should be applauded.

With so many capable women out there, I would like to see society reach a tipping point and flip, so that it would become a negative for a man not to be married to a career woman. I encourage women to choose partners who are not intimidated by strong women and who value their partners because these strong women enable their careers. I encourage women to get advanced degrees so that they can reach the heights of their professional fields. And I also encourage women to stop self-limiting themselves: Demand to have an equal seat at the table alongside men in your organizations. Once you prove that you create value, there will be no rationale anyone can use to hold you back.

It's your time. Businesses have made women's leadership one of their top priorities. They are not just pledging to increase the number of women leaders but are also setting specific goals for female representation. I don't think that we will be getting to 50/50 over the next decade, but the momentum is on your side. Go for it.

Ilene

A Word From Bram

If you are half of a dual-career couple starting out on your careers, you probably don't consider yourself deeply mired in traditional sex roles. Within your enlightened couple's cocoon, you may even think you're both beginning from a place of true equality. So, let's speak some truth about the differing baggage men and women bring to this.

Society is always banging on the sides of that cocoon, trying to enforce certain norms. In fact, most of the time society doesn't need to actually do much, because in the course of growing up, you've internalized those norms; so, you enforce them yourself.

The main social pressure that men feel is to be the breadwinner, to provide for the family, though this may have lessened somewhat in the millennial generation. If men can't do that, they may well feel like utter failures. If they succeed at that, they may feel as if every other contribution means they're going the extra mile. Women, however, are under little social pressure to be the main breadwinner. The expectation is that they should be great mothers and look as attractive as possible almost all the time. If they bring a lot of income into the family, that's gravy.

Despite the long hours of work and travel I put in during the most demanding stages of my career, I was keenly aware that I had it easy compared with Ilene. All I had to do was be the best consultant I could be and still spend time with the family, at least on weekends. Ilene had three jobs: be a great corporate executive, be a great mom and keep the family highly organized so all this could work. As a husband, you need to stay alert to ways to make your wife's life easier. You should adopt The Golden Rule here and treat your wife as you would have her treat you. You should step up and make those contributions willingly, with no resentment, glad to do your part to increase the family's happiness.[4]

Communicate honestly with your partner and be sensitive to her needs. This builds your emotional intelligence—a high "EQ" (emotional quotient or emotional intelligence) is essential for this lifestyle and brings many benefits, including making you a more effective leader.[5] In addition to EQ, you need self-confidence and a sense of humor. Be successful in your own career, which boosts your self-confidence. Sometimes society will push back. Someone will wonder why you can't go off on a guys' fishing weekend. Someone will make a remark revealing disapproval or befuddlement at your life choices: Shrug it off or laugh it off.

All this needs to be grounded in love. When your spouse needs your support, support her as she would support you. Don't compete with her. That's how my "Mr. Gordon" persona came to be (see Chapter 3, Forging Separate Professional Identities at Work, but One at Home). When accompanying Ilene to a business dinner or a conference, I wouldn't even mention Mr. Bluestein, much less toot my own horn. Sometimes this led to awkward situations, like the time at a conference when I stepped onto a bus taking all the executives' spouses on a shopping trip and found myself the only man aboard. I laughed and made the best of it.

Finally, be a good dad. That's another social expectation, and one worth fulfilling. You don't get to neglect this to further your career.

There are huge benefits to being in a dual-career couple. Besides the economic advantages, there's the potential for fulfilled lives and great happiness. You get to celebrate your own success as well as your wife's success. You will both get rewards from your work, which should result in a happier home life.

I won't say a dual career and a family is for everyone. If you aren't willing to have a spouse who has a separate identity from yours, this is not for you. If you can't support her as you would want her to support you, maybe you shouldn't even get started. As one final test, if you aren't willing to let someone other than you or your spouse raise your kids much of the time, then maybe this path is not for you. Being half of a successful dual-career couple is not always an easy path. But the most satisfying paths rarely are.

Bram

CHAPTER 1

Being the Right Partner

Bram Bluestein fidgeted anxiously, glanced at his watch and rearranged the papers on his desk yet again. He was in his late twenties, an ambitious, up-and-coming consultant at The Boston Consulting Group (BCG), working on his "qualifying case" assignment. This was a do-or-die project, a hurdle every young consultant faced—you either succeeded, opening a path to promotion, or you moved out from BCG. He was waiting for the partner on the job to come discuss what they would tell the client. The client meeting would take place in a day and a half. The partner was running late.

Bram glanced at his watch again. Fifteen minutes late. Unable to restrain himself any longer, he strode down the hall and barged into the partner's office to see what was holding him up. The partner was interviewing a beautiful young woman. He politely told Bram that he would be with him shortly. Back in the hallway, Bram thought, if I were him, I would have done the same thing.

***

Ilene Gordon was nervous. In her early 20s and preparing to graduate from MIT's Sloan School of Management, she was interviewing for a job with a partner at BCG. Well into the interview, someone shoved open the office door and stepped inside. He was tall, handsome and clearly eager for a meeting he'd scheduled with the partner. Despite her interview nerves and his restlessness, what she remembered 40 years later was that they gave each other the eye.

***

It was fitting that we first met during very important moments in our careers. It foreshadowed our commitment to each pursuing a career throughout our lives—with mutual support—while not compromising our family life.

By the mid-1970s, it was no longer a rarity for a young couple to meet at work, but in American culture it still seemed new. Only a decade before, in 1962, *Cosmopolitan's* longtime editor-in-chief Helen Gurley Brown published her famous book of dating advice, *Sex and the Single Girl.*[6] Among her suggestions for ways to meet men: while shopping in the men's department, while traveling on a plane, while driving in heavy traffic and at Alcoholics Anonymous. (She recommends a "wealthy chapter of A.A.")

***

Shortly after that meeting, having succeeded in his assignment, Bram flew to South Africa to serve BCG's client in Johannesburg. Some 16 months later, back in Boston, he crossed paths with an attractive woman in the office and eventually realized that she was the same woman he had seen in the interview. He immediately knew she was bright and ambitious—two very important personality traits to him—since she was a professional at BCG. The two of them shared the same administrative assistant, so they would sometimes run into each other in the hallway. But most of the time, consultants weren't supposed to be in the office—they were supposed to be at their client's business.

Bram later learned that Ilene had attended the Massachusetts Institute of Technology as both an undergraduate and a grad student and that she had been with the firm a year, having joined the first Monday after Bram had left. His roommate had also gone to MIT and knew Ilene well. Bram asked about Ilene and got some intel.

Then Bram was asked to speak at a Monday morning meeting, a tradition at BCG where people shared intellectual capital, to talk about living and working in South Africa. Ilene had heard about Bram while he was in South Africa. She was attracted to his adventurousness. Moving from Boston to Johannesburg and making his way in such an exotic place struck her as daring. Ilene wasn't an early bird by nature, but she showed up first thing that Monday morning and sat in the very first seat in the theater. It was midsummer, and this was the first Monday morning meeting she attended that year.

During Ilene's first year at BCG, her office mate had tried to set her up with various guys, but she hadn't clicked with anyone. She already was considered a top-tier consultant, mentored by the most important partners and widely respected. Bram had just been promoted to manager.

At that point, friends started betting on how long it would take them to start dating. It happened within a month.

LESSON: The first thing you need is that unpredictable spark. Don't overlook it when it happens. Without it, you're just spinning your wheels.

We had been flirting with each other in the office, and one hot Sunday in August 1977 Bram got confirmation that Ilene was really interested in him when she phoned: "There's a swimming pool at my apartment complex, why don't you come over this afternoon for a swim?" Bram already had plans for that afternoon, but he changed them so that he could go over to Ilene's place. It was not something he would typically do, but he was too excited about the idea of spending time with Ilene outside of work to pass up this chance.

It was normal for Ilene to reach out to men first. This is how she operated. She liked being proactive, even though she was aware that people could perceive her behavior as aggressive. Sometimes she thought she should try to hold herself back, not be so different. But in the end, she always reverted to her non-traditional approach. In this way also, Bram knew this was going to be different, that Ilene's decisiveness was part of the package of dating her: Their relationship was not going to be traditional.

Bram was not surprised that a woman was taking the initiative, but he was pleasantly surprised that Ilene invited him over. Both of them were a bit apprehensive about dating a co-worker and becoming an office couple. Bram was a bit nervous about how it would be perceived at work if he suddenly showed up with a girlfriend who was also a work colleague. Ilene had fewer hesitations. In the end, they both dismissed the matter as a non-issue, as nothing that they could not work out.

Bram felt anxious one weekend later on that summer when Ilene went off to New York to visit her older sister, a liberal-minded and politically active graduate of the University of Wisconsin-Madison and an artist in the making. (Ilene's sister would go on to become an art film director and a professor at Columbia University).

Bram was back in Boston, sitting on pins and needles, waiting for Ilene to call and say the coast is clear, come and join me in New York. He saw it as a test of how serious the relationship was getting. He thought that part of the reason that Ilene might be nervous about introducing him to her sister is because he was a straight up, clean-cut kind of guy. But then the call came, and Bram joined the Gordon sisters for a weekend in New York. Ilene's sister approved of him. Bram was relieved. He had passed the older sister test.

The courtship period lasted from August to Thanksgiving of 1977, when Bram came to Thanksgiving dinner at Ilene's parents' house. Her parents took an instant liking to Bram, especially her mother, who came to highly value Bram's opinion on everything. Bram realized he'd found a woman he was happy to be with—smart, independent, adventurous, very attractive. Someone who understood what his work was about, someone he could talk to and deal with as an equal. Someone who lit up a room. Ilene too was looking for someone smart, hard-working and adventurous, preferably with an advanced degree, as well as tall and handsome. At 24, she briefly wondered if she was too young to commit, then considered that she might not find anyone else as ideal as Bram. She knew a number of professional women who had found themselves dismayed to be still single in their mid-30s.

Another thing that appealed to Ilene: Bram, unlike so many at BCG, was not a Harvard graduate. She saw the Harvard crowd as buttoned-down salespeople, polished, connected and confident. Some came from moneyed families. Since she had attended MIT and MIT's Sloan School of Management, and Bram had gone to business school at Columbia University, they were both among the outsiders at BCG. Several people remarked that Ilene hadn't met anyone at MIT, even though the male/female ratio there was 18 to 1. Ilene would reply, "Yes, but 17 of those you couldn't even talk to."

***

Our relationship quickly grew serious. All this may sound a bit strange from today's perspective, when so many U.S. companies have strict policies about romances between employees, but four decades ago no one thought anything of it. In fact, BCG was rife with relationships back then. The consulting industry is infamous for long hours, constant travel and many divorces. At least we were both single, which made us seem a particularly licit couple.

Indeed, while the reasons companies have adopted such policies over the last few decades seem obvious, it's only honest to acknowledge that society makes some tradeoffs when it makes work romances so fraught that almost everyone strives to avoid them. For one thing, it can be difficult for people who work long hours in demanding jobs to meet someone outside of a professional context. And frequently, the more intense the work environment, the more colleagues naturally tend to bond with each other under the shared pressure. Finally, people in particular organizations or even professions may be conveniently "pre-screened" for certain characteristics. Everyone at BCG, for instance, was ambitious: i.e., hard-working, career-focused and so fiercely smart that Ilene sometimes found the atmosphere "cutthroat."

Ambition and intelligence were among the traits Ilene was looking for. She knew if she could find someone at BCG with whom she had the right chemistry, these elements would automatically be there. Bram not only struck sparks with her—he was unusually open-minded about career women for a man, even by today's standards, much less the 1970s. Given that Ilene was at BCG, he knew from day one that she was intent on a serious career.

This sort of romance would be less likely today. A 2014 global poll conducted by Monster[7] found that 39 percent of international respondents shy away from office romances, afraid that such a relationship would damage their career. Americans were the most wary of office romances, with 52 percent saying they would never date a colleague. Even Bram acknowledges that when he went on a date with a client professional, he was apprehensive that he would be found out and his career would be over.

And in February 2019, CareerBuilder's Annual Valentine's Day Survey, conducted by The Harris Poll, found workplace romances at a 10-year low, with 36 percent of workers reporting dating a co-worker, down from 40 percent in 2008.[8] Twenty percent of men admit to dating someone at work two or more times in their career, versus 15 percent of women. Yet the same survey found that, despite all the potential pitfalls of workplace romance, couples who started dating at work had a high chance of getting married, with some 31 percent tying the knot. All of which shows that if the spark exists, it is almost not to be denied.

Putting things in a larger perspective, a 2019 study published in the *Proceedings of the National Academy of Sciences* assembled data on how heterosexual couples (married, cohabiting or in romantic dating relationships) in the U.S. met from the 1930s to 2017.[9] The percentage of couples who met at work stood at 10 percent in the mid-1950s, when women entered the workforce in large numbers, and stayed around 20 percent from 1980 to 1995.

But the biggest trend here is how almost every traditional way of meeting has been elbowed aside by meeting online, which now creates some 39 percent of couples. For most of the period covered by this data, from 1950 to 2010, the number one way couples met was through friends. This plateaued at around 35 percent for decades, until 1995, when the first dating sites appeared. Online surpassed friends around 2013, and friends has now slumped to 20 percent. Meanwhile, meeting through family or in high school have both steadily declined since 1935. Meeting through neighbors, at church or at college all held steady between 7 and 10 percent for decades, from 1960 to around 2000. Ever since, every way that couples meet has declined except for online dating sites and what is now the number two way of meeting—the only other one on the upswing—meeting in bars, up to 28 percent.

This last statistic may seem curious, but clearly people are relying less on friends or various organizations to pre-screen possible mates, perhaps because dating sites are such an obvious and convenient way to screen them. Perhaps those who don't care about such screening just go to bars.

***

The two of us had much in common. Both of us grew up in middle-class Conservative Jewish households, Ilene in Newton, a Boston suburb, and Bram in Paterson, New Jersey. Our socioeconomic backgrounds were so similar that when we started dating, Bram discovered that we both had identical sets of towels from our college days, bought for us by our mothers: popcorn-style blue and white towels. And we both came from families with three children—Ilene was the middle child, Bram the youngest.

Although differences in religious or socioeconomic backgrounds are far from deal-breakers when it comes to marriage—in fact, one-fifth of adult Americans were raised in an interfaith household—most marital advice considers such factors to present additional challenges. According to a Pew Research survey, shared religious beliefs are of middling importance, cited as significant by 44 percent of respondents—way higher than agreement about politics at 16 percent (though that may well have changed since the survey was conducted, in 2015).[10] The most important factors in the survey were shared interests at 66 percent, satisfying sex at 63 percent and sharing household chores at 61 percent.

LESSON: Finding a like-minded partner who shares many of your basic values will probably smooth the way somewhat, and shared interests—whether career-related, sports, music or whatever—are very important.

Ilene's mother did some work for non-profits, but she didn't pursue a career, following the more traditional role of homemaker. She instilled the habit of serious planning in Ilene, bugging her in January about what she was going to do with her summer. "You can't just sit around for three months," she would say. She would have preferred her daughters to follow traditional paths, too, but neither one did. Still, although she worried about some of their choices when they were young, she knew better than to seriously try to hold them back.

But Ilene's father, an accountant, encouraged her. She was about 10 years old when he started asking her to help fill out his timesheets—in fact, teaching her to work with spreadsheets. She realized she was analytical and good at math. When she was in eighth grade, she participated in a math fair at her school and won. Her father drove her to the state competition. They stepped into a world full of intimidatingly smart people coming from incredible home environments. He pushed his daughter, saying, "You're as smart as these people." Later, when Ilene was accepted at MIT, he was thrilled, urging her to go for it. Her mother wondered aloud if she wouldn't be happier at a less stressful school.

Dr. Meg Meeker believes a father's influence is a major factor in the development of women. "A father has authority with a capital A," says Meeker. The author of *Strong Fathers, Strong Daughters*, she herself was inspired by her father to become a doctor. "From the first years of a girl's life, her father is larger than life. She looks up to him, and for the rest of her life she craves his admiration, his respect and his affection." Meeker says that if these qualities exist in the father-daughter relationship, they make for a successful woman.[11]

"We know what factors are related to women making better or worse income, and each of those factors is directly linked to the quality of her relationship with her father," says psychologist Linda Nielsen, an expert on father-daughter relationships. "It's her graduation rates, her interest in STEM [Science, Technology, Engineering and Mathematics] jobs, her assertiveness, her willingness to accept challenging, difficult, and scary tasks, and the sense that you're responsible for what happens to you. She gets all that from her dad."[12]

It's worth noting that studies indicate these effects are the strongest among daughters without brothers. (Ilene's brother was a few years younger and the low-key type.) Fathers may instinctually favor sons, doing girls a disservice.[13]

LESSONS:

> **• Fathers: If you simply encourage your daughters to develop their talents and strive for ambitious goals, then salute their achievements with pride, they can rise as high as any boy. If you have sons as well as daughters, beware any tendency to focus mostly on the boys—you may be shortchanging your daughters.**

• **If you're a working mom, recognize that you're a role model for your sons as well as your daughters.**

Still, for her first two years as an undergrad, Ilene assumed she'd end up as a math teacher. But she came to admire many of the women on her floor in the girls' dorm. One was on a path to become a cardiologist. Another majored in architecture, then eventually became a psychiatrist. A third, who became a lawyer, claimed she didn't care if she ever got married. Some of them were so brilliant they felt no need to study and would play bridge all night before a test. Ilene studied every night. In her junior year, when she was 20, it sank in that she didn't need to become a math teacher. She could be as ambitious as these other women. She could carve out a career in business. She could see the world. These women changed her life. Even though they were her peers, they provided Ilene with the role models she needed to see the full range of possibilities.

Donna Williamson shared an apartment with Ilene when they both attended MIT's Sloan School and has remained friends with her ever since. She describes the young Ilene as "very friendly, very determined, thoughtful. She studied hard. Very consistent, very supportive."

As for Bram and Ilene as a couple, she notes that "they always had a natural give and take, always had a sense of humor. They communicated well." She observes that both she and Ilene "just naturally gravitated to supportive males. We both had strong role models in our fathers."

Donna, who also pursued the dual-career path, was the oldest of four daughters. Her father, an engineer who worked on NASA's Gemini program and on space stations, always encouraged her aspirations, and was even criticized for sending his daughter to a private school. That was for boys.

Bram's father was a very strong figure. He came from a prominent Paterson family and his father had been a leader in the community. In fact, Bram's dad's brother and his brother-in law were doctors, setting an expectation that Bram would be a professional man. Bram's older brother followed this pathway. After being awarded his Ph.D. from MIT, he became a college professor and, then, a successful research scientist for the Lipton Tea Company.

Bram's father taught him to balance a checkbook. At a very young age, Bram would leave his father a check on the mantel for part of his weekly allowance—a nickel, dime or quarter—and his dad "cashed" it. Every month they sat down and balanced the checkbook. Bram always got it right and had allowance left over to save for a rainy day.

Bram's mother also emerged as a strong figure. She was always the optimistic person, encouraging Bram to take on challenges. She was very outspoken and was often cited in the local newspaper for speaking up at board of education meetings. Bram's mom worked, starting as an interviewer for the non-partisan NORC research organization, and was promoted to be a project manager. In the neighborhood, most of the women were "country club wives," but Bram's mom followed a different path. As she advanced at work, she grew independent of her husband, and they eventually divorced after Bram graduated from business school.

Bram was always destined to be a businessman, like his father and his grandfather before him. When he was very young, he would pick tomatoes from his grandfather's farm and sell them door-to-door in the neighborhood. When Halloween came, he bought a box of candies and sold them individually in the neighborhood at a profit. And he was always at ease in the front of the room leading weekly youth services.

In addition, he was always comfortable with strong women. His grandfather would say, "Behind every successful man is a successful woman." Bram's grandmother was his grandfather's bookkeeper, and she was self-taught since women weren't encouraged to pursue much education at that time.

Bram's older sister was his closest female influence when he was a kid. Eighteen months older than Bram, she is responsible for his name, which he has used all his life. According to Jewish tradition, Bram was named for a relative who had passed on. In his case, it was his grandfather, Abram Isaac Bluestein, who had died at the age of 59, not long before Bram was born. Unable to pronounce the full name, Abram, his sister started calling him Bram. His grandmother, heartbroken after the early death of her husband, who was known in the family as Abe, lit up when she heard the name Bram.

Growing up, Bram had a strong relationship with his sister, who he describes as "one of these older sisters who got her way." While the three siblings were all close, the brother went off to private school when he was in his sophomore year of high school, and Bram and his sister spent three years together as the only two kids in the house. That time helped bring them together even more, and they remain very close to this day. Bram considers her to be a strong and successful woman.

She graduated from the University of Miami and moved with her husband to Thomasville, in southern Georgia, where she had a successful career as a real estate broker and became an ambassador for her community. She helped bring a temple to Thomasville. She also joined the Rotary Club and rose within the organization to become a Rotarian Governor, leading half the Rotarians living in Georgia.

Bram has naturally worked well with strong women, starting when he was an assistant to a woman commissioner at the Federal Trade Commission before joining BCG. At BCG Bram always worked well with women colleagues on different assignments.

Right from the start, Bram had two key ingredients for a man in a successful dual-career couple: Be strong and successful in your own career, and be comfortable that you have fallen in love with and married a woman who is as strong as you and enjoys being independent. But even Bram admits that he wouldn't understand the next two ingredients for a while: Build your relationship on the principal of parity, and recognize the feedback you get will frequently be based on traditional norms.

In fact, in research published in 2018, based on surveys of 100,000 people across 29 countries, Harvard Business School Professor Kathleen McGinn and colleagues discovered that sons of employed mothers hold significantly more egalitarian gender attitudes about the sexes in the workplace—even more so than daughters of stay-at-home moms.[14] They also tend to marry women who are employed, and they spend a bit more time on average than other men caring for family members—perhaps a result of growing up watching their mothers juggle so many tasks. (The research also found that children of working mothers end up just as happy in adulthood as children of stay-at-home moms, and daughters of working mothers tend to have more successful careers than daughters of non-working mothers.)

How ahead of his time was Bram in 1978? Consider that business bible *Forbes.com* ran a story in 2006—or 27 years after Bram and Ilene started dating—titled "Don't Marry Career Women."[15] The article started with the following words of wisdom for men: "Guys: A word of advice. Marry pretty women or ugly ones. Short ones or tall ones. Blondes or brunettes. Just, whatever you do, don't marry a woman with a career."

Quoting significant research studies, *Forbes* then listed all the miseries that marrying a career woman may lead to: "If a host of studies are to be believed, marrying these women is asking for trouble. If they quit their jobs and stay home with the kids, they will be unhappy (*Journal of Marriage and Family, 2003*). They will be unhappy if they make more money than you do (*Social Forces, 2006*). You will be unhappy if they make more money than you do (*Journal of Marriage and Family, 2001*). You will be more likely to fall ill (*American Journal of Sociology*). Even your house will be dirtier (*Institute for Social Research*)."

Presented with this article, Bram bridled at the conclusions, wondered whether the research cited had missed the point and rejected the idea that he was looking for trouble when he started dating Ilene. "If a dominating husband imposes his will on a wife who wants to work, insisting she stay home, of course she'll be unhappy," he notes. "You can't be that dominating husband when you have a career wife. Would I be unhappy if Ilene made more money than I do? I think most of the time those differences are not material. When they do become material is later in life when, if you have a good marriage, you celebrate the success. You're both happier because you get to do more together than if you had less income."

Expressing skepticism that he'd be more likely to fall ill and his house would be dirtier, he suggests, "get a Roomba, let a robot do the floors." He muses that many of the values implicit in these studies change over time: "We may even be at a tipping point, where people feel that if you can have two careers in a family, you'll be happier."

Ilene weighs in: "Who's going to bring out the best in you? That's what the best marriages are. Bram brought out the best in me." And Bram says the same is true of Ilene.

LESSONS:

• **If you're looking for a husband who will be half of a dual-career couple, make sure early on that he's open to this and will be supportive of your own career. You can improve your odds by focusing on men who grew up with a working mother or a number of strong women in their family.**

• **If you are looking for a wife who will be half of a dual-career couple, make sure early on that her intent is to have a career. You have a better chance of succeeding as a couple if she is starting with that intent, rather than your counting on it to develop over time.**

Although men still hold the top positions in most organizations, women have made a lot of progress in moving up. According to the U.S. Bureau of Labor Statistics, women now occupy at least half of professional and management positions, outnumbering men as accountants, financial managers, and medical and health services managers, for example.[16] And while women were the primary earners in only 18 percent of marriages in 1987, that number was up to 29 percent in dual-income marriages by 2014.[17]

According to Pew Research, in the U.S., in almost two-thirds of couples with children, both partners work and the number of dual-earner couples is increasing.[18] As Jennifer Petriglieri, an associate professor at INSEAD (Institut Européen d'Administration des Affaires), notes, "Many of these are *dual-career couples:* Both partners are highly educated, work full-time in demanding professional or managerial jobs, and see themselves on an upward path in their roles. For these couples, work is a primary source of identity and a primary channel for ambition."[19] Sociological research indicates that such couples have certain advantages besides the economic ones—including a more satisfying relationship and a lower-than-average chance of divorce—as well as facing a distinct set of challenges.

Shauna H. Springer, Ph.D., thinks two of the main reasons well-educated couples tend to have better marriage outcomes are a longer courtship period and an older age.[20] These couples date an average of 3.6 years before their wedding and are in their late 20s to early 30s—more than three years older than average—when they marry. Such couples also tend to agree that it's wise to spend some years getting established in their careers before having children.

Dr. Thomas R. Lee of the Department of Family and Human Development at Utah State University agrees that a longer courtship and being older both improve the chances of a successful marriage. Parental approval of the intended spouse also helps. Additional important factors include a willingness to compromise, common interests and good communication.[21]

LESSON: No need to rush anything. Being a bit older (late 20s or early 30s) and having a long courtship both increase the odds of a long and happy marriage. For a dual-career couple, spending several years establishing a career before having children usually makes sense. It helps if both of you have established a track record at work, proved your value and earned some flexibility. And try to pick a partner your parents approve of, if possible—less drama and stress.

We dated for four or five months, then Bram was asked to move to the Munich office. BCG was looking to beef up its European presence and was encouraging employees to relocate. Ilene seized the opportunity to move to London, and Bram quickly maneuvered his way to London instead of Munich. Then, we moved in with each other.

In fact, rents in London were so high that we soon decided to buy an apartment—the first major life decision we made together. In true BCG style, we drew up a contract, because Bram had the capital and Ilene had the income. Bram would later joke that, when we sold that apartment, we made so much money on it—and the contract was so complicated—that we had to get married.

Our time in London was high-flying. During the brief hours we weren't working intensely, we played hard. We liked to go to a nightclub called the Dial 9 Club and dance the night away, a new experience for Bram. We went to movies, especially thrillers and spy movies. We gambled trivial amounts at London's private-club casinos.

After a year in London, Bram was invited to help open a new office in Chicago. BCG offered to create a position for Ilene there, too. As fun and interesting as London was, Ilene had discovered to her surprise that the UK business world in the 1970s looked down its collective nose at Americans, especially American women. We were both ready to move on, but Ilene had one condition: "If we're moving to Chicago, we have to get married on the way."

During a trip back to the States as we prepared to move to Chicago, Bram officially proposed on Valentine's Day and we immediately went shopping for rings. The 21st was considered a lucky day by Bram's family, thanks to a number of birthdays and anniversaries on that day. The only 21st's that might work were in April and July, but July 21st was Ilene's birthday, and she didn't want an anniversary on her birthday. So, they planned a wedding in two months.

Ilene liked the idea of pulling together a wedding in only two months because she was a career person and the office in Chicago needed to open up. She felt she didn't have time to spend a year on engagement parties and all that "fussing around." She always wanted to be different. So, she thought, "*I want to get married, but we'll do it the career way.*"

Back in December, we had already bought tickets for a March trip to South Africa, so we decided to consider that pre-wedding vacation our honeymoon. We had to be a little flexible to make the wedding happen in two months. There's a room in Boston's Copley Hotel where Ilene used to take dance lessons as a kid: She wanted to have the wedding there, but we had to be out of that room by 6:45. We were concerned the rabbi might run long with the ceremony, but he assured us that he had to do another wedding later that evening. All the rooms for drinks after the ceremony were taken, so we had drinks by the hallway staircase, which has a lovely view from the top, then moved to another room. So, we made it work, and after a great wedding, we flew to Chicago.

LESSONS:

• If you want to date someone at the same company, check on the company's norms re professionals dating or being married to each other. It's only natural to meet people at work when you spend most of your time working, but this is a potential minefield, and power imbalances at work can affect relationships. If such a relationship becomes serious, it may even make sense for one or both of you to consider changing firms. Keep your job separate from your personal life to the extent possible—and leave work at the office. Believe it or not, support groups exist for work colleagues who are dating each other. If there's one in your community, join it if you can.

• If you aren't a dual-career couple yet, there are some specific markers that should help you ensure you are on track to be successful. If you are a dual-career couple, consult these lessons and adapt them to your own life. And be confident that you *can* have two careers and a family: Our relationship is evidence for that. (Read the rest of the book.)

CHAPTER 2

Finding the Right City

SO, we were married at the Copley Hotel in Boston on a Saturday night, arrived in Chicago Sunday night and were the first two employees at the BCG office on Monday morning. One flight attendant on the plane to Chicago thought we were so cute that she gave us a bottle of Champagne to take with us!

We thought we would be in Chicago for a few years before we moved to another city for BCG. In those days, there were no well-pronounced trends toward "mega cities," or lists of great cities to live and work. We were just lucky that it all worked out. Let us share what we learned along the way and how it helped us to be successful as a dual-career couple.

At first, we imagined we'd spend a couple of years in Chicago and probably end up in New York at some point. As much of a major city as Chicago was, back then many people on the East Coast still thought of it as a cow town full of steakhouses. In fact, there's a pretty good concentration of headquarters of Fortune 500 companies within striking distance of Chicago—a concentration that has only grown over the past decades to a few dozen corporations. It was like finding an undervalued stock that would only get better. And the city has become ever more cosmopolitan. We ended up falling in love with Chicago and eventually realizing that it was a great place to raise our kids.

Currently, Chicago boasts 34 Fortune 500 headquarters in its Metropolitan Statistical Area, second only to New York City with 71. And according to Numbeo, Chicago has the 24th-highest cost of living in the Americas, lower than Boston, Philadelphia or St. Paul/Minneapolis.[22]

Although the world is now full of lists of the best places to live and work, including such specialized rankings as the best places for newlyweds, single millennials and even ex-pats, no one has yet produced a list of best cities for dual-career couples. While we won't attempt to create a comprehensive list here, we can suggest some obvious places that are worth a deeper look.

According to the McKinsey Global Institute's 2019 report, "The future of work in America," 25 "megacities" and "high-growth hubs" and their peripheries could account for 60 percent of job creation through 2030 even though they include only 44 percent of the population.[23] The pandemic has no doubt reshaped this somewhat, giving certain types of workers more flexibility about where they live, but most job creation and economic dynamism will likely still revolve around cities.

McKinsey's megacities include Atlanta, Boston, Chicago, Dallas, Houston, Los Angeles, Miami, New York, Philadelphia, Phoenix, San Francisco and Washington, D.C. High-growth hubs include Austin, Charlotte, Denver, Las Vegas, Minneapolis, Nashville, Orlando, Portland (Oregon), Raleigh, San Antonio, San Jose (Silicon Valley), Seattle and Tampa/St. Petersburg.

Meanwhile, for a different and global perspective, there's Mercer's Quality of Living 2019 city ranking.[24] (Like everything else, this list has been upended by 2020 and Covid-19, so much so that Mercer is not issuing a 2020 ranking.) U.S. cities on the list include San Francisco, Boston, Honolulu, New York, Seattle, Chicago, Washington, Philadelphia, Pittsburgh, Minneapolis, Dallas, Atlanta, Houston, Los Angeles, Miami, St. Louis and Detroit (in order, from number 34 to 72 in the ranking). A number of Canadian cities outrank all the American ones: Vancouver (tied for number 3),Toronto, Ottawa, Montreal and Calgary.

In case you're looking for international experience farther afield, the top 20 on this list are dominated by Western European cities, especially in Switzerland—rather expensive—and Germany, with a sprinkling of cities in Australia and New Zealand. Vienna ranks first for the tenth year in a row. The top-ranked Asian city is Singapore, followed by some half-dozen cities in Japan.

And Citrix ShareFile's 2017 Businesswomen Power City Index lists the top 20 cities for women in business, ranking cities based on factors like number of executive jobs held by women, female-owned businesses, female buying power and wage gaps between men and women.[25] This doesn't necessarily correlate with best cities for dual-career couples, and some findings may surprise you. (Baltimore ranks first for businesswomen. Tampa and Washington, D.C., both included on McKinsey's list, come in second and third.)

But when we first moved to Chicago, there were very few women professionals, especially in senior positions. Ilene was one of the first. She was something of a pioneer. But she never fretted about whether working women would be accepted. She assumed she'd always be a pioneer. Somehow, Ilene always made it work.

We were struck by how affordable Chicago was, especially in terms of real estate. Even now real estate costs two or two-and-a-half times as much in New York or Boston. Later, we learned that childcare was also affordable and that the schools were quite good.

Another big advantage of Chicago was that the area is easily drivable. So you can live in the suburbs and drive without too much grief into the city. For a while, we lived downtown and drove out to jobs in the surrounding area, or even further afield.

Travel on a broader scale is also important. When we were working at BCG in Boston, we noticed that every time we flew to the Midwest we had to change planes in Chicago. We hate changing planes—from Chicago you can fly nonstop most anywhere. So we made sure to always live within an easy drive of O'Hare Airport, thus reducing the stress of frequent travel.

Another factor that matters much more for some people than others is sports. Chicago has a number of major league teams. Despite coming from Boston and New Jersey and, therefore, growing up following Boston and New York teams, we soon embraced Chicago sports teams despite all the heartache that switching allegiances entailed (with the exception of the Bulls in the Michael Jordan era). It was a great way to bond with our kids when they were growing up.

LESSON: Find a city with plenty of opportunity for both of your careers to thrive. If you want to work in the corporate world, or consult for it, a profusion of corporate headquarters makes sense. Or if one of you is a doctor, for instance, you'll want some top hospitals in the area. Fortunately, most cities with a high concentration of one or two industries—Houston for petroleum, Los Angeles for entertainment, New York for Wall Street and media—are large enough to provide good opportunities in a range of fields.

Ilene was always a Bostonian deep down, and she loved New England. But after she met Bram and they had the opportunity to go to London, she knew that she was ready to leave. She loved her family, but they were very tight-knit, and she didn't want to feel stretched by family expectations. She didn't want to move to New Jersey and feel obligated to see Bram's family for Sunday brunch every week. And she knew the experience of London and dealing with European companies would be broadening and, thus, important for her career. When Ilene told her parents she was going to London, they weren't surprised—they'd always known that Boston was too small for their daughter.

When people ask Ilene what she gave up in order to have her career and her family, she readily replies it was an active social life: "You only have 24 hours in a day, seven days in a week. Something's gotta give." So, if you're the sort of person who feels the need to throw a dinner party every week, the dual-career life might not be for you.

In fact, American families tend to be fairly spread out. A 2012 survey conducted for AARP by Lake Research Partners found that while 71 percent of parents age 50+ have children living within an hour's drive of them, 40 percent have children living more than five hours away.[26]

LESSON: Weigh carefully the pros and cons of staying close to family versus establishing a buffer zone. There will be family obligations, and these may increase over time. And assuming your extended family is centered in

your hometown, you'll probably also have a wide circle of old friends there. While most of us love seeing family and friends, if you're working long, intense hours or are constantly on the road (as consultants, for example, tend to be), you may want to reserve whatever weekend time you have for your spouse and children. So, approach this matter with open eyes. Only you can decide what kind of balance works for you. But be aware: There always will be tradeoffs and guilt trips.

For Ilene, going to London was a way of breaking out of Boston. She loved the fact that it was a high-energy, very global city. Years later, in her corporate life, she would draw on lessons learned there and encourage employees to seek international experience. Nowadays, when someone says they're moving to Europe, Ilene advises, "do Asia, or else you're not challenging yourself. Europe is too easy now." And she offers up this rule of thumb: "If you haven't learned how to do your own laundry in a foreign country, it doesn't count as an international experience."

But in the 1970s, being a career woman in London was tough, and not just in the business world itself. When Ilene applied for a credit card at department store Harvey Nichols, she was rejected, essentially for being a single female, who thus they considered unstable. It didn't matter how much money she made. Back in the States, Ilene wore her experience in London proudly, like a badge of honor.

Over the past few decades, many multinational companies have made international experience a requirement before someone can be considered for a top post such as chief financial officer or CEO. And a 2017 survey about the academic backgrounds of CEOs at the world's largest companies by study choice portal Study.eu found that almost a third of them spent time studying abroad during their university years—some five times the general average of 6 percent.[27]

Moreover, a series of studies have demonstrated that living abroad—not just traveling abroad—enhances creativity.[28]

Also, writing in the *Harvard Business Review*, a group of researchers describe "How Living Abroad Helps You Develop a Clearer Sense of

Self."[29] They focused on "self-concept clarity," which "has been linked to a host of benefits, such as psychological well-being, the ability to cope with stress, and job performance." Essentially, people living abroad are forced to grapple with cultural differences, which helps them sort out which of their values and norms are instilled by their culture and which are their individual core values. This develops a clearer sense of self, which leads to clearer career decisions. The researchers showed that developing this clearer sense of self is linked to the length of time spent living abroad but not to the number of countries lived in.

> **LESSON: Be adventurous. Get some international experience and, if you can, get comfortable living in a new culture. Obviously, it's usually easier to do this before you have children, maybe even before you get married.**

Throughout your career you will be offered positions that may require relocation. U.S. norms are changing, but being in the right community was pretty important for most of our careers. Whenever these opportunities come up, the decision is more complex for the dual-career couple. For the move to be attractive, it needs to increase the career opportunities for both partners, not just one.

At one point, Bram was offered an interesting opportunity in St. Louis. He could head up strategy and join the executive committee of a major corporation. He was starting to get excited when the executive recruiter asked, "What about your wife?" The recruiter spent a couple of weeks investigating possibilities for Ilene, then he called Bram and explained that opportunities for her were very limited—she was already too high-ranking an executive. So Bram turned down St. Louis.

Americans now move about half as often as they did in the 1950s, according to Census Bureau data, a rate that's been declining for decades. According to Axios, "the rise of dual-career couples has contributed to lower mobility rates between cities and has made it harder to recruit workers to smaller job markets....This is one reason for the growing concentration of high-paying industries and jobs in just a handful of booming cities. Dual-career couples tend to cluster where they both have job security—not just in their current jobs but with options to jump elsewhere in the same market."[30]

LESSON: If either member of a couple feels they have to put their career on the back burner—or even on hold—for the sake of the other, resentment will build, even if it smolders beneath the surface. Do everything you can to avoid this situation.

Some years later, during the 1990s, Bram was working for another consulting firm, A.T. Kearney, and they moved him to the Southfield, Michigan, office, just outside Detroit. Ilene had observed that whenever she met someone from Detroit, they expressed a desire to move to Chicago, and she had no intention of moving in the opposite direction. So, Bram began a serious commute that would last some eight years.

The flight to Detroit was only 40 minutes long and cost $65 each way. This was before 9/11; so, airport security didn't take too long. Bram was a morning person; so, he didn't consider it a problem to get up at 4:30 every Monday to catch a 6am flight. If one of their children had an event during the week, such as a school play, he would fly back for it. When Bram was done with his week in Detroit, on Wednesday or Thursday, he'd fly back home. If he had to be in the office on Friday, he'd usually do that as a daytrip. So, some weeks he flew back and forth three times. Eventually, he bought a car in Detroit and left it at the airport parking lot every weekend—with a fresh change of clothes in the trunk.

After the Detroit era, Bram did a longer commute (two-hour flight) to Dallas for a couple of years. It was during these commuting years that he came up with a rule for himself: Never walk into a cold house. This meant that as soon as he climbed into his car and left the airport for home, he called Ilene. This allowed them both to catch up, switch gears and, if necessary, vent about their day. They would chat for about 15 minutes, until Bram was sitting in the driveway, asking if he could hang up and come in.

Still later, between 2006 and 2009, when the kids were in college, Ilene embarked upon a truly extreme commute: to Paris. She ran a $6.5

billion global packaging business for Pechiney, a French company that was owned by Alcan Aluminum, and one of the requirements was that she had to have an address in Paris to get a work permit. When she was offered the job, the company asked her to move to Paris—and to decide within two days. Such a major decision was too quick, even for Ilene. So, she turned down the offer. The company soon called back with a counter offer, saying, "If you commute to Paris for a year, we'll pay for your apartment, and then you'll have to move." Bram convinced her to go for it, that they would make it work. If they had to move, Bram's firm would be happy to relocate him to Paris, so that wasn't a problem. Before the year was up, Rio Tinto bought the company. They didn't care about packaging, because they bought Alcan for the metals business. So, they asked Ilene to keep commuting and help them sell the packaging business.

Ilene developed a system. Chicago to Paris was a good flight, long enough to sleep. And the time difference between Paris and Asia, where many of the company's packaging facilities were, was only seven or eight hours. So 11 times a year—excepting August, when no one in France is in the office—she flew to Paris for a week, then to Asia for a week, then back to Chicago for two weeks. Bram also developed a system: To keep the lines of communication open, he would call Ilene three times a day.

Danielle Lindemann, assistant professor of sociology at Lehigh University and author of the book *Commuter Spouses: New Families in a Changing World*, has done intriguing research into couples in such situations, finding that their relationships often remain quite strong even as they challenge traditional gender expectations.[31]

Previous research has found that when one spouse relocates because of the other's work, the woman is usually the "trailing spouse." But the commuter couples she studied did not prioritize the husband's career over the wife's. And, most encouraging of all, about a quarter of Lindemann's respondents said the separation had drawn them closer or made the relationship more interesting. In fact, these couples say they value their marriages and families at least as much as couples who live together.

Megan Bearce, a marriage and family therapist and author of *Super Commuter Couples*, has identified factors that help such a commuting situation work.[32]

Members of such couples know how to manage "re-entry," the family transitions when one spouse returns or leaves. (Bram's rule about not walking into a cold house is a good example. Ilene also developed a rule for her Paris commute, which was to adapt to the time zone immediately.)

These "super commuter couples" also stay connected and are good at closing "intimacy gaps" that arise from physical separation. (Bram talking to Ilene three times a day when she was in Paris is one example.)

LESSON: While extreme commutes certainly present challenges, for the right opportunity, you shouldn't dismiss this out of hand. Instead, consider the benefits both to your career and your family's financial future. Many couples become quite good at managing their "distance marriages," and some even grow closer as a result.

CHAPTER 3

Forging Separate Professional Identities at Work, but One at Home

Soon after Ilene started work at BCG, a nameplate appeared on her door: "Miss Gordon." Bristling, she marched into Human Resources and demanded a new one that read *Ms.* Gordon. She didn't see why her professional identity should be tied to her marital status. Unruffled, the HR staffer shrugged: "Sure, no problem, it only costs a dollar." Within a day, Ilene's new nameplate materialized on her door.

For the first eight months of our marriage, Ilene didn't change her name because she wanted a separate name at work. But then she legally changed her name to Bluestein on her Social Security card. Bram didn't pressure her to change her name, but society did. Ilene had this dream that she could be Gordon at work and Bluestein in her private life. What she didn't realize was that when she was changing her name with the Social Security Administration, she was bursting her own bubble.

A couple of years later, she was working in the packaging division at Tenneco and considered a high-potential employee. But Human Resources drew up the organizational charts by payroll, and Ilene was being paid as Bluestein. So, the charts they put together for an HR review listed Ilene as Ilene Bluestein and not Ilene Gordon. At the meeting, the CEO, who was considered a godlike figure, asked, "Who's Bluestein?" Told that this was Ilene Gordon, he said she had to choose one name and couldn't have it both ways. When this news got back to Ilene, she quickly changed her Social Security ID back to Gordon.

The tradition—in English-speaking countries and much of Western Europe—that women take their husband's surname is rooted in English common law. (The situation is different in much of the world, including most Spanish-speaking countries, China and among most Muslims.) Women were considered property of their fathers, and thus bore their father's surname. When they were literally "given away" at marriage, they were relabeled with their husband's surname.[33]

In the U.S. changes away from this tradition have remained relatively slow and sporadic. While 23 percent of brides in the 1990s kept their maiden name,[34] by 2011, this was down to 8 percent, with 86 percent taking their husband's name and 6 percent hyphenating or creating a new variation, according to a survey by TheKnot.com.[35] "Some researchers speculate that women may now be rebelling against the 'hassle' of hyphenated names or differing last names that they saw growing up," according to Dorie Clark in the *Harvard Business Review*.[36]

Yet, brides who are established professionally are more likely to keep their surname.[37]

LESSON: It's important to establish separate careers with separate identities, especially early on, and a name is a very visible symbol of that identity.

As Bram started to attend dinners and other business functions as Ilene's spouse, it dawned on him that he was there to support her. He noticed that other husbands there in the same situation would often sit in the corner and sulk, while others would stand side by side with their wives and compete for attention. He determined that he would stand side by side and support her.

After a while, he decided he might as well have a little fun with the situation. So, he started introducing himself as Mr. Gordon. This became his alter ego within Ilene's business world.

It's important for a man to understand that there is this other role to develop, a role in which you support your spouse as opposed to supporting or promoting yourself.

Within Bram's consulting world, spouses would come to monthly partner meetings and dinners. And Ilene would be there as Mrs. Bluestein on behalf of Bram. Much later, when she was a CEO, she became less Mrs. Bluestein and more Ms. Gordon, since people wanted to know about the company she was running.

She would also use Mrs. Bluestein to try to blend in with the other spouses who didn't work outside the home. Professional women were comfortable with one another, but they tended to be a small minority at these events, and they were often given the cold shoulder by the other wives.

LESSON: You should learn to set egos aside and support each other in turn. When the evening belongs to your spouse, don't step all over it.

Spouses often compete about work, according to marriage therapists. They may be in the same field, having met at work or grad school. In any case, when couples work in the same field, raises and promotions can provide grist for rivalry.[38] And research shows that we are most envious of those who are close to us, according to Abraham Tesser, distinguished research professor emeritus at the University of Georgia, who is known for developing a psychological theory of envy.[39] Pursuing different careers can help a couple, because it makes competitive comparisons more difficult.

The relationship has to be a mutual and equal partnership, and one important aspect of that is giving each other good career advice. That can be a big advantage for a dual-career couple. Spouses in single-career families will also tend to advise each other, but a non-working spouse's counsel may not carry as much weight or credibility as that of a spouse who is "in the fire"—that is, engaged in the working world day to day.

In fact, the ideal situation for a couple advising each other is when they both share some familiarity with a particular industry or profession, or at least the corporate world in general. Two lawyers, for example, will be plugged into networks that may well overlap somewhat. They may have dealt with relevant law firms or heard professional gossip that might shed light on the wisdom of a particular career move. But while a couple that includes a lawyer and a doctor can still offer each other useful advice in general, they very likely cannot advise each other on law firms or hospitals.

LESSON: Whatever your situation may be, there is an unbreakable rule: Never make a decision concerning a job without involving your spouse.

Sometimes you may feel you know what's best for your career and think it would be easier to just decide on your own. This is almost always a mistake. It's vital to engage your spouse in a discussion about such a decision, even if in the end you agree to disagree. All this decision-making can be hard—that's one more reason it's important to have a certain passion for each other.

After we were married and living and working in Chicago, Ilene announced that she wanted to leave consulting for the corporate world. For one thing, we wanted to have children, and she knew that two consultants in one family with children would be challenging because of the hours involved, the amount of travel and the lack of control over your schedule. Consultants tend to work around 70 hours per week versus 50 hours for corporate executives. And consultants are very focused on their clients—if a client says he needs you there tomorrow, you show up tomorrow. While on the corporate side, if someone wants you to travel for a meeting and you say, "I can be there next week," no one raises an eyebrow. Corporate people travel periodically but, generally, not every week, although the amount of travel tends to increase in more senior positions. If we both were consultants, it would be too hard to start a family.

In 1974, sociologist Lewis Coser coined the term "the greedy professions" to describe fields that "seek exclusive and undivided loyalty," jobs like consulting, law and top managerial positions. And today, long hours have become common in more and more white-collar jobs.

As Harvard economist Claudia Goldin told the *New York Times*: "'If you put in the extra hours, if you're around for the Sunday evening discussion, you'll get a lot more [money].' To maximize the family's income but still keep the children alive, it's logical for one parent to take an intensive job and the other to take a less demanding one, she said. 'It just so happens that in most couples, if there's a woman and a man, the woman takes the back seat.'

"Women don't step back from work because they have rich husbands, she said. They have rich husbands because they step back from work."[40]

Taking on such unequal roles is something that Bram and Ilene simply refused to do.

Moreover, Bram had a passion for consulting, and he was very good at it. He loved analyzing problems and strategizing how to fix them. Ilene felt she was just an average consultant, and she was eager to get more involved in actually managing a business, implementing changes and executing strategy. On top of all that, Ilene's move out of consulting and into corporate management would eliminate any direct competition between them.

> **LESSON: It's best if you're not competing directly with each other. Bram was five years older than Ilene, which was helpful in this respect, since he was already one more rung up the career ladder than she. Working in different fields or industries also can help.**

Bram didn't try to talk Ilene out of making a career change. He recognized that Ilene's personality and skill set were suited for the corporate world, that she would be happy there and that the move made sense. So, they set out together to find the right opportunity for Ilene, immediately using their knowledge of their clients to become educated partners for each other.

The job search took some time. Ilene was one of a relative handful of professional women, but hiring one wasn't considered a triumph at the time, and as a consultant, she was paid very well. Eight months after arriving in Chicago, Ilene made the jump to the corporate side of things, starting in a planning position at Signode Corp. (later bought by Illinois Tool Works), which entailed a half-hour reverse commute into the suburbs. Signode was a Fortune 500 company that manufactured strapping systems, which opportunely built on what Ilene knew about packaging from her consulting work.

Combining consulting and corporate careers was enhancing for us as a couple. Ilene wasn't escaping to a completely foreign world: From a consultant's point of view, she was just moving to the client side of things. It was the next step in her career, and it made our relationship more dynamic.

> **LESSON: Every decision has to work for both the individual and the couple, and it must be made together. In this case the decision suited Ilene's talents and interests, and it enabled the two of them to start their family.**

After more than seven years at BCG, Bram moved to the consulting firm Booz Allen as a partner and spent another seven years there. One of his clients there was the retailer Montgomery Ward, whose CEO worked hard to attract Bram to the company.

Bram surprised his Booz Allen colleagues by accepting a position at Montgomery Ward and spending a year or so on the corporate side of things. This new experience was a transformative point in his career. When Bram was starting out as a consultant, he was evaluated on how well he solved a problem, how well he communicated the solution and, thus, how easy the solution was to adopt. At Ward he realized how consultants effectively leveraged executives' limited time to accomplish what they really wanted to achieve. So, he emerged from that experience with a greater sense not only of how important it was to solve a problem but also how to leverage a client's investment in achieving implementation.

It was every consultant's dream to land a senior position in corporate strategy, but Bram quickly learned that the grass wasn't any greener on the other side. Retail is a tough industry, and Bram found himself working even more intensely than he had as a consultant and growing restless.

Back in those days, Ilene would drag Bram out of the office by coming by in the evening to pick him up. One evening, Bram climbed into the car and said, "Guess what? I got a call from a recruiter today for a firm called A.T. Kearney. They're looking for a partner to head up their North American strategy business."

Ilene responded, "Oh my God, they'd be fantastic!"

"What do you mean?" Bram asked.

"I know them," she replied. "They're a consultant of ours. We're doing a lot of work with them. They're great people, good thinkers. They do great operations work. You should be open-minded."

"Really? *Hmm.*"

Ilene was conducting herself as an informed, caring partner. She sensed that Bram would be a good fit at Kearney, and she also wanted her "old husband" back, the one with the cheerful consultant's personality.

Bram ended up going to Kearney and staying, happily, for 17 years.

A.T. Kearney had an annual bonus program; every January, you would start on a new page. So, every year, the questions to be considered were, how was Bram doing? Should he stay at Kearney and keep on consulting? And every December, during their warm-weather Christmas vacations, Bram and Ilene would spend time in the pool, away from the kids, talking. Ilene would listen and advise, trying to make sure Bram was reading the metaphorical tea leaves correctly.

And in turn, based on his knowledge of companies gleaned through consulting, Bram would advise Ilene about opportunities she was assessing in the course of her career.

At one point, when Ilene was commuting to Paris for Pechiney, the CEO asked her if she would become the firm's chief financial officer. Ilene, who was basically operating on high school French, doubted whether her language skills were good enough for that position, but the CEO tried to convince her she could do it.

She was flattered to be offered such a high-ranking position, and she certainly did not lack confidence. If she had felt that being CFO would someday lead to a job as CEO, she would have jumped in and done her best to make it work. (So, this was not an instance of the classic self-doubt many women feel when offered more responsibility, in contrast to the frequently unjustified confidence that men exude in similar situations.) But Ilene was already running a business, and she was convinced that a profit-and-loss line position offered her a better path to CEO than a staff position, even a high-level one, in finance or strategy would.

Research shows that Ilene's intuition was correct, although the finance route to CEO is far from impossible. In fact, most up-and-coming CEOs assume significant roles in operations, often running the most important division, before becoming CEO. Some three-fourths of Fortune 100 CEOs came from operations. The other main route is through finance: Almost a third of Fortune 100 CEOs previously held the position of CFO.[41]

When she called Bram with this news, his reply was, "If they think you can do it, you need to think about whether you agree with them. They're trying to create an opportunity for you." Meanwhile, he wondered to himself whether Ilene could make it work since she wasn't trained as an accountant and her French was less than fluent. But he never expressed those reservations to Ilene. He knew she was perfectly aware of those facts. As a spouse who was a true partner, he saw his role as helping his wife think through her decision, not as sowing doubts.

So, Ilene and Bram discussed and dissected the offer thoroughly over multiple conversations. In the end, Ilene felt confident and comfortable with her decision, because the two of them had hashed it out. She stuck to her guns, turned down the offer and stayed on her path toward CEO.

LESSONS:

• **When it comes to making career decisions, dual-career couples have both shared and individual responsibilities. You are responsible for your own career moves, for helping your spouse with their career, and for considering what's best for the family. Taking into account your spouse's perspective will help you make better decisions for your own career. So, even though your career is your responsibility, you always should make career decisions together.**

• **Decide on your identity early on, and how separate or integral it will be professionally and personally. This is a** function of the nature of your relationship over the course of your marriage. The stronger the push for a separate identity, the stronger the odds that you will have successful dual careers.

• Learn to support each other. The big advantage dual-career couples frequently have is the ability to empathize with the challenges their partner is going through at work. Helping each other sometimes requires that a husband learn how to be "Mr. Gordon" and have fun doing it.

CHAPTER 4

Building Your Family Becomes Your Priority

Just like any happy parents, when our daughter, Emily, was born we wanted to send out a birth announcement. In the pre-email days, our only choice was to have the announcement printed and mailed via the U.S. Postal Service. Rather than resort to the traditional format and order a boilerplate announcement from a local print shop, we decided to create a unique proclamation. It included the traditional information but, based on our consulting experience, we formatted it like a business chart, using the concept of a "Happiness Curve"—because adding Emily to the family was a very happy event.

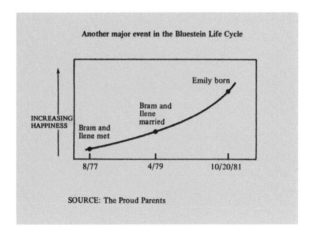

DOUBLING DOWN

When Andrew was born, we created our second very-happy-event birth announcement. Not only were we increasing our happiness, but we found that adding Andrew initiated a sense of balance in our family. Both Ilene and Bram grew up in families with three children, and when we were young and imagining a future family, we both tended to picture what we were familiar with: three kids. But once Ilene got her career going, we decided two would be enough.

In fact, when Ilene delivered Andrew and was told the baby was a boy, she started to cry. A nurse asked her if she was okay. Ilene replied, "I have a boy and a girl, I'm done!"

You can see the fun we had with the Happiness Curve through the three-page birth announcement below:

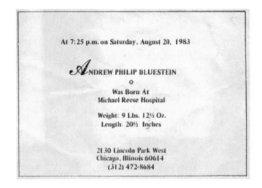

At 7:25 p.m. on Saturday, August 20, 1983

ANDREW PHILIP BLUESTEIN
◇
Was Born At
Michael Reese Hospital

Weight: 9 Lbs. 12½ Oz.
Length: 20½ Inches

2130 Lincoln Park West
Chicago, Illinois 60614
(312) 472-8684

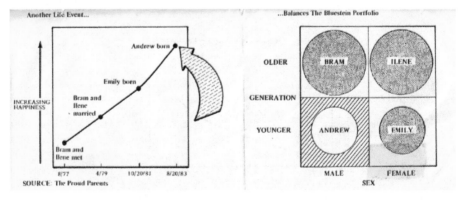

48

By initially wanting three children, just like our parents had, and eventually settling on two, we followed the generational trends. According to Statista, the average number of children per woman was already down to 2.33 by 1960, fell below 2 in 1978 (to 1.96) and was around 1.87 in the early 1980s.[42] In 2019, the average reached 1.93. To reach an average of 3.0, according to a CDC study, you have to go back to the generation of women born around 1935.[43]

Ilene grew up in a very traditional home where her father did not do household chores and her mother cooked every day. Her mom taught elementary school during the first few years of her marriage, then took a break to raise the kids. Afterward, she went back to teaching young children, didn't like it so much, took a job in medical records, then jumped to retail—which she loved—working at Filene's—Boston's equivalent of Macy's. Ilene's mother was driven by wanting to have her own source of income more than wanting her own career.

Ilene's parents always expected their kids to be conscientious about schoolwork and go to a great college. Over time, Ilene internalized those expectations, and her ambition grew. She wanted the best career, the most money, the most success. She wanted more than her parents' middle-class life. Some families in her hometown of Newton were more prosperous: The kids went to private schools, the families took better vacations and belonged to country clubs. Ilene wanted that life.

Her parents believed in the virtue of blending in. There was safety in not drawing attention to yourself. Neither Ilene nor her sister were concerned about that. They were happy to stand out.

But Ilene's mother held out hope that, eventually, her two daughters would become more similar to their parents. When Ilene was 28 and told her mother she was having a baby, her mother replied, "You're not ready." She imagined Ilene would have to take a break in her career to raise kids. She had never known a woman to keep working with young children at home.

In fact, the share of all mothers who were stay-at-home mothers with working husbands stood at 40 percent in 1970. By 2012, that number had drifted down to 20 percent, having bottomed out around 17 percent in 1997.[44]

Bram was more inclined than Ilene to replicate the life he had grown up in: a Conservative Jewish family with strong bonds and an emphasis on education. He grew up in the suburbs with a full-time housekeeper and he assumed that he and Ilene would move to a suburb after[their first child was born. In the end, he did more or less replicate that life, with a couple of big twists: He spent much of his life traveling, becoming a citizen of the world, and Ilene became CEO of a Fortune 500 company.

This last "twist"—being part of a dual-career power couple with a family throughout our whole marriage—is what makes us truly unique. Having children (usually more than one) is what most typically drives many professional women from the workforce, whether they opt out or are pushed out (and often it is very difficult to determine the difference between these two reasons), thus eliminating one of the two careers among dual-career couples.

In 2013's *Lean In*, Sheryl Sandberg notes that "43% of highly qualified women with children are leaving careers or off-ramping for a period of time." She also observes that this entails a serious penalty: "Only 74% of professional women will rejoin the workforce in any capacity, and 40% will return to full time jobs."[45] The complete truth is even harsher, as virtually none of those full-time jobs will be as high-powered or high-paying as the jobs these women were seemingly preparing for in their 20s.

One of the unusual things about Ilene was that she saw this harsh reality clearly at the time. She had no illusions that the business world would wait for her if she took a few years off, and she was determined to avoid the situation that derails so many women—trying to re-enter the workplace in her 40s and having to settle for whatever job she could get.

Another way she stood out: Among women in the 10 highest-paying occupations in 1980, only half were married and only a third had a child, according to research by Marianne Bertrand, an economist at the University of Chicago Booth School of Business.[46]

Indeed, the company Ilene was working at when our first child was born had never had a professional woman on staff before, let alone one with a baby. Yet they were supportive.

A 2015 study by UCLA's Robert Mare showed an increase of assortative mating: Spouses are more likely to have similar levels of education than they did mid-century in the U.S.[47] Many people assumed that societal change was leading to a proliferation of power couples. But two writers reached out to the sorority sisters they had graduated with at Northwestern University in the early 1990s to see how their careers had turned out.[48] Their research indicates that power couples are quite rare: "Of the 39 women we graduated with who are either married or partnered, only 4 fit the classic power couple description: A chief marketing officer at a bank married a corporate real-estate vice president; a sought-after screenwriter married a music executive; a wealth manager at a large investment bank married a brokerage executive; and a prominent doctor married a general counsel at a brokerage firm."

Most of these women married men with equivalent degrees. But after children entered the picture, one spouse decided to stay home or found a flexible or part-time job that allowed them to be the main caregiver. In some cases, both spouses scaled back their ambitions and responsibilities—forgoing a promotion or a chance to make partner, for instance, in exchange for more time with the family. But almost all the highest-achieving women married men who dialed back their careers or became stay-at-home dads.

LESSON: You can have two active and successful careers, but it's not easy. Paradoxically, to make this work, family must become a priority: Your family becomes your most important job. The balance of this chapter lays out key aspects of how we did it.

When we had our first child, Emily, Ilene took three months of maternity leave. Our parents came to help during the first few weeks, but we also hired baby nurses early on.

Breastfeeding was a lot less popular than it is now. Research since then has shown that it's better for the child, and many people look on a failure to breastfeed as unfortunate, which is why companies now have rooms reserved for mothers to pump their milk. But none of that was expected in the early 1980s, and the two of us had to split the work. So, we decided to bottle feed.

Ilene remembers when she was still in the hospital and a nurse knocked on her door, offering to teach her how to breastfeed. Ilene sent her away. She wished she had a sign on her door that said "Professional Woman."

We soon hired a live-in nanny. We invested in an apartment that was large enough for a live-in nanny, which was a significant expense. We considered it an investment in Ilene's career.

Many people balk at the thought of giving up privacy with live-in help, but everything in life involves tradeoffs. We found this one worth it. Besides, after you have children, what kind of privacy do you really have? Other couples choose to rely on family members for help with the kids, but that entails another tradeoff in terms of availability and reliability. Better to use grandma as a backup nanny in case, for example, your professional nanny has a dentist appointment.

If you can put together a backup support system and make it work, more power to you. Ilene once met a woman whose children stayed at a daycare center that closed its doors at six o'clock. The woman had put together a network of parents as backup. So, when she was held up late at work, she would text one of these parents a few minutes before six and ask them to pick up her kids. Ilene admired this woman's organizational abilities and determination to create a backup childcare system that worked—and wishes that texting had existed back in the 1980s when she was organizing our children's schedules.

Because she did not have a cell phone in the 1980s, Ilene's organizational prowess was sometimes subverted and things went awry. She especially dreaded the month of May, when Chicago's heavy rains could change the kids' school activities and also complicate transportation. One time, there was a miscommunication between Ilene and the nanny that left our kids standing on the corner in the rain, waiting to be picked up. Ilene was very upset when that happened, and it took her some time to calm down after the mishap.

Our first nanny was a very warm woman who had previously worked for a cousin, but who spoke only Spanish. (Our cousin spoke some Spanish too.) We spoke no Spanish at all, so we communicated with sign language. But in the long run, that wasn't sustainable. We also had some issues with boundaries. Essentially, we wanted to be the parents on weekends. Our nanny had weekends off, but she was living with us seven days a week, and she didn't have many outside interests. She tried to take care of Emily and Andrew on Saturdays and Sundays. But we were committed to being hands-on parents on weekends.

The second nanny we hired had actually received formal training as a nanny, and she was fine. She made herself scarce on weekends.

Our third and final nanny, a Filipina named Cindy, was with us for some 16 years; so, clearly she was great. Cindy shared an apartment with her brother and, therefore, went home on weekends. When we moved out to the suburbs, at first she'd come out on the train because she didn't drive. She'd grown up in the Philippines in an era when most women didn't learn to drive. This wasn't the best situation. We tried to hire another nanny, but had trouble finding someone who was as good a fit with our family as Cindy.

So, we offered to teach Cindy to drive. She said that would be great and that she had a friend who could teach her if we paid the same rate as a driving school, and we agreed. Soon, we bought a third car for Cindy's use, something safe and utilitarian like a Honda or Toyota Camry. We maintained the car and paid for gas, and Cindy used it to drive the kids around, then took it home on weekends.

To this day, Emily thinks of Cindy as her second mom and is still in touch with Cindy as well as with some of Cindy's friends.

"Delegating" some of the childcare to nannies or babysitters has, of course, been a contentious issue, although public opinion has grown more supportive of working mothers over time. In 1977, Pew Research's General Social Survey first asked if a working mother "can establish just as warm and secure a relationship with her children" as a mother who stays home: Only 49 percent of American adults agreed. That share climbed to 70 percent in 1994, then dipped into the low- to mid-60s. Since 2008, the share of U.S adults who believe that a working mother's relationship with her children is just as warm and secure as a stay-at-home mom's has stayed above 70 percent.[49]

Yet Americans also believe that having a parent at home is best. In a recent Pew Research survey, 60 percent said children do better when a parent stays home, versus 35 percent who said children do just as well with working parents.[50]

LESSON: You will quickly realize that you can't do it all yourself. You must build a support system that fits your lifestyle.

While we wanted our nanny to take weekends off—we liked spending a lot of time with the kids and making it clear that we were the parents—we soon realized that we also needed some weekend help. For one thing, the two of us were determined to spend time with each other on Saturday nights, and sometimes Friday nights, especially since Bram was usually traveling during the week.

Those Saturday nights together, strengthening our relationship as a couple, were good for the children as well.

Research shows that children in high-conflict families, regardless of whether the couple is intact or divorced, do worse than children of parents that get along, according to a study review by Robert Hughes Jr., professor and head of the Department of Human and Community Development in the College of ACES at the University of Illinois.[51]

After casting about for some time, we eventually found some reliable teenage girls to handle babysitting on the weekends, so we could go out on Friday and Saturday night. Saturday during the day we'd often be running around with Emily and Andrew. These girls were all very sweet, and they were happy to earn a little money.

There were other organizational tasks that required some creativity to arrange. Ilene didn't want our kids sitting at home playing with the nanny all day just because she was working. She felt they needed to interact with other people. So, shortly after we moved to the suburbs, Ilene signed Andrew up for a preschool course. This was a five-minute drive from our house, but our nanny didn't drive yet. Ilene got a list of all the parents of kids in the class and called them one by one, saying, "I have an offer for you. If you pick up my child, you can leave your child with my nanny and have your afternoon free." Three or four people hung up on Ilene before one woman said, "Sure, I'll do that." The woman would pick up her son and Andrew, drop off both boys at our house, where they would play while our nanny kept watch, and the woman would run errands or whatever and pick up her son at around three. So, it was a win-win all around.

Looking back today, Andrew remarks, "Mom was CEO of the family before she was ever CEO of a company."

Being the CEO of a family is an often unheralded and under-appreciated position, and women tend to do more of it than men. Men devote 18 percent of their time to housework and take on 33 percent of household tasks, while women spend 22 percent of their time on housework and shoulder 67 percent of household tasks—twice as many as men. Women also take on the planning and coordination of tasks.[52]

However, for Ilene, planning came naturally. "Mom would start planning the next vacation while you were still on vacation," remembers Emily. "She always likes to be a step ahead and aware of everything. She used to plan what's for dinner every day with Cindy, and now, when she takes Andrew's kids for a Saturday once a month, she also plans ahead all of the meals and activities."

When Emily was born, Ilene took three months off, then started a new job at another part of the packaging company. When Andrew was born, almost two years later, Ilene was itching to get back to work, largely because her job was in danger of being taken over by someone who wasn't distracted by children—a common hazard for working mothers. Ilene took only one month off.

Companies that shortchange working moms are short-sighted, to say the least, yet this is extremely common. According to Bright Horizons' 2019 Modern Family Index, a survey conducted by Kelton Research, a staggering 89 percent of American workers say working moms in leadership roles bring out the best in their employees.[53] Moms excel at multitasking, managing conflict, listening and keeping a level head in a crisis, so this does make sense.

Yet the same study found that 72 percent of those same workers believe women pay a penalty at work when they have children, an issue that doesn't apply to men. Sixty percent say employees who are less qualified than working moms are offered leadership positions. And 41 percent of workers see mothers as less dedicated to their careers, despite their high ranking as leaders.[54]

LESSON: Having a family makes you better at work. You will be more organized, clearer about priorities, and generally more empathic.

The first few years of parenthood, we split a lot of the childcare duties. We'd get home from work around seven, and the nanny would retreat to her room. We'd have a takeout dinner and then say, "Let's divide and conquer." We'd each take one child to put to bed. Bram would always take Andrew, read him a story, tuck him in, and Andrew was asleep in three minutes. Emily would ask for several stories, then insist that Ilene stayed until she fell asleep. Ilene wasn't about to leave Emily to cry, making her feel guilty about her mothering. When she finally emerged from the bedroom, Bram would say, "I've been out here for an hour."

Even on the weekend, when the kids were giving them a hard time, Bram would go off with Andrew and Ilene with Emily, which made things easier. Divide and conquer.

On Saturday mornings, Bram would often take both kids out for breakfast, making a point of keeping them away from the house long enough for Ilene to sleep in. During the summer, Bram spent many Sundays swimming in the backyard pool with the kids. And later, when the kids were in high school, Andrew became quite a good golfer. Bram would take him golfing regularly (and usually lose).

When Ilene and Bram cooked, they also divided and conquered the dishes, with Bram grilling and Ilene preparing a salad. "As chefs, they were good enough—not outstanding," remembers Andrew, himself a great and passionate chef.

Lack of clarity in the division of chores between working spouses often leads to resentment. According to a 2007 Pew Research poll, sharing household chores was in the top three issues associated with a successful marriage—third after faithfulness and good sex.[55] Some 62 percent of adults said that sharing household chores is very important to marital success. In 1990, only 47 percent of respondents said the same. No other item rose in importance so much.

LESSON: Share parenting with your spouse. Your number one priority is in your own home. But remember: Your

partner faces the same challenges with free time and energy that you do.

At one point, Bram was serving as coach to Emily's basketball team. They had a game coming up, and Bram got delayed on a business trip. Realizing he'd never be able to fly back in time, he called Ilene with the disappointing news.

"Don't worry about it," she replied, "I'll go coach them."

Bram pointed out that Ilene knew nothing about coaching basketball, but she shrugged off his concern. "I'll make it work."

Before the game, Ilene approached the coach of the opposing team and suggested a scrimmage. He agreed, and both teams experienced a great practice session.

She made it work.

LESSON: Find creative solutions. Think outside the box. With enough determination, you will find a way.

Sunday night dinner became a Gordon-Bluestein family tradition— it was when all four of us all got together and caught up with one another. We would all go through the schedule for the upcoming week, including the kids' schoolwork. This was when Ilene passed along the habit of planning that her mother had instilled in her. If either child had a project due in a week, we would check on the progress. Ilene insisted that the children not start a school project the night before it was due—they had to start working on it the month before.

It was about teaching them always to devote their best effort to their schoolwork. "The expectation was do you best, get your work done, try the hardest," says Emily.

Andrew recalls that his mother would sometimes get overinvolved in his papers or ask too many questions. In fact, it was only after he got to college and no longer ran his papers by Ilene that he realized he had lost his toughest—and, therefore, his best—editor.

Ilene herself thought of Sunday as "homework jail," the day when her kids' assignments occupied her for most of the day.

Indeed, at the start of her professional life, Ilene bought a little red scheduling book from *The Economist.* Every year, she bought a new one and kept track of her professional life in it for years. Eventually, her scheduling book included not only her business meetings but also due dates for the kids' papers, projects and spelling bees.

Every Sunday dinner ended with cupcakes, a treat the kids always looked forward to.

We also made a point of always taking vacations with the kids, another family tradition that helped us all regroup and catch up.

Ilene liked kids to participate in activities with other kids. That's why she registered Andrew and Emily for a sleepaway summer camp. Emily liked roughing it, sleeping in tents and using porta-potties. Andrew, however, was not so keen on camp. He would have preferred to stay at home with TV and air conditioning. One summer when he was 10, Andrew was packed off to a sleepaway camp. During the parents' visit after the first four weeks, Ilene told her reluctant outdoorsman that he'd be staying for another four weeks, something Andrew hadn't been aware of. Ilene did it for her son so that he would not be bored at home. But she also did it for herself, so that she could have a less taxing summer schedule.

To this day, Ilene regrets ambushing Andrew the way she did. "It's the only time that I made my son do something that he didn't want to do," she says. And while Andrew now brings up the situation as a joke, more to tease his mother than because he is holding a serious lifelong grudge, Ilene still feels guilty about it.

LESSON: Create family traditions. Stay engaged.

We both prioritized family and tried to be available to our kids. When Ilene was in Paris, she would take her kids' calls during business meetings. She used a flip phone as long as it was feasible, because it fit discreetly in her pocket, where she could set it to silent and feel the buzz when she got a call. She didn't make a big deal about having to take a call from one of her children—if the meeting was important, she would wait and call back later. But in a routine meeting, she would step out of the room and answer the call. She knew the kids weren't calling just to chit-chat. They needed help with a school paper or some sort of advice.

She also traveled with a set of spelling-bee flash cards with the grade-appropriate words whenever Emily was about to take a spelling test. Ilene would sit in the back of a car, traveling from a business meeting to dinner, and go over each word with Emily on the phone. "She tried to be there even if she wasn't there," says Emily. One time a taxi driver turned to Ilene and said, "I see that you're mothering from the back of my cab."

LESSON: Do not shortchange your kids just because you have to work; be available as often and as much as you can.

When Andrew got into Cornell, we were all thrilled. He made the waitlist at MIT, Ilene's alma mater, and they called Ilene to ask, "Does he really want to attend MIT?" She asked Andrew outright, and he replied, "Not really." So Ilene said, "Well then, don't go." And Andrew ended up loving Cornell. Parents who become fixated on their children attending the same school they did as a legacy are being rather selfish. Remember, finding the right school is about your kid, not about you.

When Andrew played basketball in middle and high school, Ilene would attend the games. But once he became a serious golfer, she refused to attend his matches. Mostly, she was afraid she'd make him nervous and maybe cause him to miss a shot. Golf is a mental game, after all. Partly she found it stressful because she was too nervous herself.

And confidence is vital for success. Children need to be empowered to lead their lives. Bram gives credit to his uncle, a very bright, successful radiologist. When Bram was a boy, he used to clean his uncle's office to make a little pocket money. One day, his uncle asked him if he wanted to be a doctor. Bram replied that he wasn't sure he was smart enough. His uncle said, "You're smart enough to do anything you want to."

That simple belief stuck with Bram, empowering him to go off and take on the world. He chased success. And in his mind, success meant education, financial security and love.

Emily and Andrew both realized that their parents were unique. Most of their friends had stay-at-home moms, and they certainly did not have live-in nannies. While Emily and Andrew wished their mother and father could be home more often, they also appreciated that their parents were always there for them.

They saw it wasn't always easy on Ilene and Bram. "Mom had to show everybody at her job that she could do everything that a man could do," says Emily. And Bram would literally go out of his way, flying back from another city just to attend school events. They taught their children grit by example.

In 2013, University of Pennsylvania psychologist Angela Duckworth won a MacArthur "genius" grant for her research on a powerful, success-driving personality trait called "grit."

Defined as a "tendency to sustain interest in and effort toward very long-term goals," her research has correlated grit with educational attainment, grade-point average in Ivy League undergrads, retention in West Point cadets and rank in the U.S. National Spelling Bee.[56]

Our kids created their own lives and careers, which in some ways resemble ours and in others are very different.

We see more of Ilene in Emily. They look similar, and Emily has definitely inherited Ilene's organization gene, her impatience and matter-of-factness. That organizational skill was quite evident when Emily started to build BEA Real Estate Enterprises from nothing. Emily had the whole process planned out: First she acquired a one-bedroom apartment, then she remodeled it using a general contractor, then she rented it out for a year at a time. Emily developed standard processes for each step in the process and reviewed them with both of us before implementing them. While Emily gave us the opportunity to comment on her processes, she had already figured out the most efficient way and she would always defend doing it her way. Emily now owns more than half a dozen one-bedroom units in Chicago.

Emily started off her career as a teacher—with a degree in education from Lynn University in Boca Raton—following in the footsteps of Ilene's mom. After a decade in education, she was burning out, but she was not interested in the world of big corporations that her parents had inhabited. Instead, she started her real estate firm. While initially not business-oriented, Emily has turned out to be a good businesswoman. Together with Bram, she deals with the need for housing repairs or tenants' requests and complaints. Emily is very thoughtful and has a good business brain, says Bram. Ilene likens managing apartments and buildings to working in education, because dealing with tenants requires some of the same negotiation and peacemaking skills needed when dealing with students.

Andrew is more like Bram in terms of body type and personality traits. He is smart, logical and analytical, yet not as quick to make decisions as Emily or Ilene.

Bram admits to having aspirations early on for Andrew to follow him into consulting. Andrew started his career at a consulting firm, where he impressed his bosses with his smarts from the beginning. While still an intern, he was asked to look at some forecasting models that the firm had created for a client. Andrew noticed that while all the data sets seemed relevant, the model would make more sense if the cells of the spreadsheet used to build the forecast were divided by each other rather than multiplied. His future employers were impressed and agreed with his assessment. He got the job, and the company paid for him to get a graduate business degree.

Even though he was successful as a consultant, Andrew did not enjoy the traveling lifestyle as much as Bram once did, especially since Andrew was starting a family and eventually became a father of two. After his consulting firm merged with another one, bringing in thousands of new colleagues but losing a sense of professional comradeship, Andrew left consulting. He first tried private equity, but did not find the transition to be a natural progression. So, he settled on venture capital, which, according to Bram, fits Andrew like a glove.

At Bluestein Ventures, a venture capital firm that "invests in the future of food," Andrew is one of the cofounders (with Bram). He is the firm's chief strategist, an area of business he finds exciting, the way Bram did. Son and father now discuss potential investments when they meet entrepreneurs who want to develop the next-phase burger to revolutionize health. Ilene serves as the "guru," a final sounding board for entrepreneurs, who are half-jokingly advised on the firm's website that she holds people accountable.

All this is about teaching your children to imagine—and commit to—a future they want to create.

As he once did on Saturday morning with his kids, Bram now takes his grandkids for breakfast or lunch when they spend a weekend with their grandparents. And while Ilene has the course of the weekend all planned out, she admits that she and Bram serve as traditional grandparents.

With more time on our hands, we're available to play with the grandkids. And we spoil them a little, the way all grandparents do, leaving the disciplinarian role to the parents.

LESSONS:

• **Support/empower your children. You have to know who your kids are and what is going to make them feel happy and successful.**

• **Build a support system that fits your lifestyle. In our case, we used a live-in nanny as the anchor of our system. Knowing that our children were being well cared for while we were at work allowed both of us to pursue our dreams with a lot less guilt. Even if this requires spending all or most of one spouse's earnings, when you're working in a lucrative field, hiring good, reliable childcare is an investment in your future earnings. And if your passion involves working in government, say, or at a non-profit, it's an investment in your life satisfaction. We made it our number one priority.**

• **Never forget that your children are independent people, not extensions of you. When they make major decisions, offer advice, but leave your ego out of it.**

CHAPTER 5

Walking the Tightrope of Work-Life Balance

When we were starting out in our relationship, the term "work-life balance" literally was not part of our vocabulary—or anyone else's. The term originated in the 1980s in the U.K. as part of a plank in the Women's Liberation Movement platform, calling for flexible schedules and maternity leave for women.

We weren't consciously focused on any sort of balance but, intuitively, we soon realized we had to implement certain measures to have a life together.

This led to our first rule, established while we were living in London: The Saturday-Night Rule. Bram was commuting to Sweden much of the time to work with a client there. One day he called Ilene and explained that it would really simplify his life if he stayed over in Sweden for the weekend. Ilene objected to the separation—if they didn't spend time together on the weekend, when would they? So, she flew to Sweden for the weekend.

From then on, whenever Bram was in Sweden, either Bram made the effort to fly to London on the weekend or Ilene flew to Stockholm. What began on a whim became formalized as our Saturday-Night Rule: Barring truly extreme circumstances, we would make sure to spend every Saturday night together. And in 40 years of marriage, we've spent perhaps 10 Saturday nights apart.

The very act of preparing for date night helped us to re-engage in our relationship. Making yourself presentable to your partner is the first step in this process and causes you to think about how your partner would receive you. What we did on these nights ranged from going to the movies to dancing or black-tie benefits and always included dinner. This was essential to allow us to separate from the day-to-day stresses of our jobs. We instinctively knew that these events were essential to keeping the romantic side of our relationship alive and healthy.

Research shows that regularly planned date nights in a couple's schedule can boost emotional connection, friendship and sexual desire—all vital factors in a happy relationship.[57] Yet many couples neglect this chance to fortify their bond. Excuses for not bothering to build in regularly scheduled time for each other include the expense of a night out, exhaustion from a hard workweek, the problem of finding a sitter, and the hassle of planning the evening.

But if anyone had a fistful of potential excuses to blow this off, it was us. We simply made spending quality time together a top priority.

Considering the amount of business travel in our lives, this wasn't easy. Once, for instance, when we were living in Chicago, Bram was in Colorado and had to stay for a partner meeting and dinner scheduled for Saturday. Ilene flew to Colorado and joined him for the dinner. Another time, when Bram was on the management committee at A.T. Kearney, he spent a few days in Australia for a regional meeting. He had to leave by 3:30pm on Friday to catch an overnight flight in order to be home Saturday. So, 3:30 rolled around and Bram simply announced, "I'm done. I'm leaving." The CEO frowned and asked, "Where are you going?" Bram replied, "I have an eight o'clock dinner in Chicago tomorrow that I have to make." And he made it home for Saturday night.

To us, consciously carving out time from our demanding schedules to spend together was worth it, even if we didn't have research to back us up. But it turns out that if you're in a good or long-lasting relationship, the mere presence of your partner boosts your happiness level, according to a University of Minnesota study published in 2016.[58] The research followed 47,000 married couples over seven years and came up with literally feel-good findings: When someone is with their spouse, they are twice as happy on average, and they rate their activities as more meaningful.

We came to appreciate the rules we adopted as pre-negotiated solutions. Trying to negotiate a new solution every time a situation comes up is tedious and exhausting. Far better, whenever there's a difference in approach or priorities between members of a couple, to settle on a compromise or solution that covers that general situation, especially if that situation is recurring. Like Saturday nights. Having pre-negotiated solutions in place—aka "rules"—creates a game plan for your marriage that sets expectations and eliminates much of the stress.

In effect, your rules become a formal statement of your priorities.

Bram used to tell his teams that, compared with his wife, he had an easy job. He appreciated the challenges she faced dealing with a couple of extra stakeholders during the week and juggling her various roles: trusted advisor to Bram, corporate executive, mother and wife. This awareness made it easier to develop the rules and implement them rather than endlessly debating what the rules should be.

Some of our rules evolved organically as routines that became expectations and, therefore, didn't require much enforcement. We've already mentioned how Bram would take the kids out to breakfast on Saturdays and keep them out till 10am so Ilene could sleep. That's one example.

Others were a bit more complicated, like the 48-Hour Rule.

Consulting is a particularly intense work environment, and it's very easy to give up a weekend at home for work. If you give up two weekends, you're on a slippery slope. You quickly get into the habit, and before you know it, you're away almost every weekend, with no time for your family or even yourself. When you start down this path, you're living on adrenaline, but you can't keep going like that forever. There's a high burnout rate and a high divorce rate in the industry.

Many clients seem to have a habit of scheduling meetings early on Monday morning. An 8am meeting would force Bram to fly to Detroit or Dallas on Sunday night rather than catching a 6am flight on Monday morning. One weekend, Ilene said, "You know, if you leave home on Sunday, you're really cutting the weekend in half." "How so?" Bram asked. "You spend the whole day Sunday thinking about leaving instead of enjoying the weekend."

Bram conceded that she had a good point. After some discussion, we settled on the 48-Hour Rule: We had to spend a full 48 hours at home on weekends before taking off again—unless we negotiated a special exemption. This constrained us somewhat on either Friday evening or Monday morning, but there was flexibility built into the rule, and it assured us of two high-quality weekend days every week. Bram got into the habit, whenever a client scheduled an 8am Monday meeting, of asking a week in advance, "Could you push that meeting back to 9am?" Clients would say, "Sure, no problem."

Pretty soon, the kids figured out that 48 hours was two days, and they became major fans—and enforcers—of the rule.

LESSON: Make your own rules to fit your own situation. Rules are helpful: They minimize stress by providing pre-negotiated solutions.

The biggest obstacle to maintaining your work-life balance is other people. They will make demands that stretch your life out of shape—it's your responsibility to set limits and learn how to say *"no."* Our biggest challenges were staying away from people who would throw roadblocks in our way and finding people who would accept us and even help out. The most helpful were usually people dealing with similar challenges and ambitions. We have some great friends, going back decades, who we might have dinner with twice a year, and who understood that we couldn't do it more often. But we still feel very close to them.

Other people sometimes will become allies in this respect. Ilene had a great boss at Tenneco, who would insist she left early enough on Halloween to take her kids trick-or-treating. This is an example of the impact your direct supervisor can have on your life. Don't expect all bosses to consider such things.

When we were young, companies were just starting to implement a few policies aimed at women or working moms, but not really anything for dual-career couples. We didn't let the policies—or lack of policies—get in our way. We just pushed the envelope and asked for what we needed. (When you ask for something, make sure to offer an easy solution, like Bram asking a client far in advance to postpone a meeting by an hour.)

At the same time, we wanted both our careers and our family, but we tended to almost hide the family. We didn't want any special dispensation. So, Ilene wouldn't announce, "I have to take my daughter to a doctor's appointment." Instead, she'd say, "I have a commitment at three o'clock," and hardly anyone ever questioned her further.

Of course, to ask your boss for what you need and get it, you have to produce. You have to add value. If you do that consistently, people will notice and respect that. This is far better than simply putting in long hours and making yourself always available to work. And it's just one reason it makes sense to spend five years or so establishing yourself in your career before starting a family—by then, you should have gained a reputation as a valuable employee.

It's not always easy, or even realistic, for companies to establish blanket policies that promote work-life balance, especially if they do business globally. If companies declare no meetings after 5pm, how do they deal with Asia? It's better to be flexible. Don't wait for companies to institute policies, just ask for what you need—and make sure you're valuable enough that your firm wants to keep you happy.

Of course, companies sometimes delude themselves about the satisfaction of their workforce. In a 2015 study by *Workplacetrends.com*, 67 percent of HR professionals said that their employees *were* achieving work-life balance, but only 45 percent of employees agreed.[59]

And the concept of work-life balance has evolved since the 1980s. According to the *2015 EY Global Generations Survey*, "Work-life balance has shifted to incorporate both the issues and strategies aimed at effective time management for employees. It has also expanded to include burnout prevention and stress management....There is increasing emphasis today in making work-life balance more gender neutral."[60] In fact, men now say they are more willing than women to change careers (60 percent men, 52 percent women) or forgo a promotion (57 percent men, 49 percent women) to help manage the demands of family and work.

(One intriguing generational difference: In light of the fact that the U.S. is the only developed country without mandatory paid parental leave, 38 percent of millennials say they would "move to another country with better parental leave benefits" versus 28 percent of Gen Xers and only 11 percent of boomers.)

Sometimes you also have to ask your children or your spouse for some help or some latitude. Invite them into your world. When Ilene had to travel for a meeting, for example, she didn't treat the meeting as a mysterious event, where the kids had no need-to-know. She would explain in simple terms what the meeting was about and why it was important for her to be there. The kids accepted this.

As our Sunday night dinners became established as a family tradition, that became a sort of corollary to the 48-Hour Rule: Both of us were supposed to be there. Exceptions required negotiation. For instance, one time Ilene had to go to a five-day training session in Texas, a couple hours' drive outside Houston. The session kicked off with a dinner on Sunday night. So, she asked Bram if he could watch the kids Sunday night, and he said, "Sure." Most people heading to the training session were catching a 1pm flight from Chicago, but Ilene didn't want to miss the whole day—the 4pm flight would be better. So, she called the people running the training and let them know she'd be there Sunday night but would miss the dinner. (One rule of thumb from Ilene: It's better to arrive at a long meeting late than to leave any meeting early.) Then Bram made the "ultimate sacrifice" of driving her to the airport for the 4pm flight, bringing Emily along. This gave mom, dad and daughter an extra 45 minutes together before Ilene had to say goodbye.

> **LESSON: Don't wait for companies to come up with rules/policies to help maintain work-life balance. Be proactive: Make sure you're a valued employee, and make your needs known. Be professional, open and flexible. You have to embark on a mission to balance your own life and career.**

The part of consulting that requires the most time is serving clients—luckily for Bram, that was the part he loved. The travel involved was a necessary evil—always done off the clock, mostly at night—that ate up a lot of time. The actual work shifted with growing seniority: Young consultants would solve problems for clients; more senior ones would write proposals selling the work, network and build relationships to ensure a steady stream of business. Some consultants loved the administrative side of things, or rather the power that the administrative side gave them.

Bram loves solving problems, giving presentations, the pressure to perform. So, he let the administrators handle their side of things, and he handled the consulting. That seemed to work well. His only "work hack" was maintaining clear priorities, which allowed him to focus on what he enjoyed doing. The same principle applied to the family.

Earlier, Andrew remarked that Ilene was CEO of the family before she was CEO of a company. Bram notes that Andrew failed to mention that Bram was the household's chairman of the board. Bram enjoys making policy and formulating rules but has no interest in administrative details, such as paying bills, something that Ilene enjoys doing. This led Bram to a "life hack"—he applied the theory of comparative advantage to home life: Do what you enjoy and are good at.

If you like paying bills, pay the bills. If you like buying the food, do the grocery shopping. We never attached sexual stereotypes or value judgments to our roles either. When the kids were young and Bram was watching them, he wouldn't hesitate to change diapers. A task is a task is a task. And as long as we tended to do what we enjoyed, switching off with each other when necessary, life went more smoothly. So, while we had a high-performance work model, we also developed a high-performance life model.

> **LESSON: For a high-performance life, ignore sexual stereotypes. Split responsibilities equitably and use the theory of comparative advantage (but not in regard to earnings): Do what you enjoy and are good at (and hope that, most of the time, these are one and the same).**

If you want to live a dual-career family life and succeed, organization and time management are key. Fortunately, Ilene has always been extremely organized, good at compartmentalizing and a compulsive planner. She hates wasting time.

So, she would pop out to a nearby store on her lunch hour to stock up on diapers rather than stop to buy them on the way home from work. That way, she would get home as quickly as possible and have a bit more time with the kids before dinner and bedtime. When on a flight for business, she would look around at all the business travelers seizing the chance to read a novel and shake her head. Who had time for fiction? She read novels only when on vacation. On a business flight, she would pay the bills—by check. Even after it became easy to pay electronically, Ilene enjoyed writing checks.

Another key advantage—if possible to arrange—is living close to work and schools. For most of the time that we lived in the Chicago area, we lived in the suburbs, and Ilene also worked there. In case of emergency, she was a mere 20-minute drive away. One day, she got a phone call: Emily had fallen off her bike, and an ambulance was taking her to a hospital that was 10 minutes from Ilene's office. Ilene proudly beat the ambulance to the hospital. She immediately called Bram in Detroit and told him he needed to come home. Three hours later, he was there. (Emily turned out to be fine.)

Another family tradition that evolved into a rule was taking vacations with the kids, which helped us all reconnect and stay happy. We quickly became big fans of Club Med, since it was the first resort to provide babysitters and activities for the kids. In her usual organized/planning mode, almost as soon as one vacation was over—as soon as Club Med opened its registration, 11 months in advance—Ilene would make reservations for the next vacation.

Obviously, we both became skilled at juggling a lot of responsibilities—especially Ilene, who was stretched in more different directions much of the time—but we succeeded at this by avoiding multitasking in the strict sense (that is, constantly interrupting your focus to check emails or answer the phone). The real key is to prioritize your tasks clearly, organize your day, and maintain that discipline.

The better way to focus? Batch your tasks, grouping similar sorts of work together so that you stay in a similar mental mode for blocks of time. Set aside specific times of day to check email, and train your contacts to not expect an instant response. Try to schedule phone calls in advance to minimize random interruptions. Schedule your day so that you tackle the most intense tasks when you're at your most energetic and focused. Try to alternate intense work with less intense tasks.

The dark side of multitasking has been amply documented. It leads to a drop in productivity as high as 40 percent.[61] You may think you're multitasking, but the human brain processes one task at a time—you're just switching rapidly between tasks.[62] And this makes you slower and sloppier. People who are interrupted and switch their attention back and forth take 50 percent longer to accomplish a task and make 50 percent more errors.[63]

Don't try to do everything yourself. Delegate tasks to specific staff members. When appropriate, ask them to document their steps so that you develop a written procedure that anyone can follow. Hunt down and eliminate wasted time and effort. Focus on one issue at a time.

LESSON: If you want more balance in your life, get organized. Maintain clear priorities. Stay disciplined.

One key skill we both mastered over the years is efficient business travel. As we write this, people are more focused on productive Zoom meetings, but vaccines are becoming plentiful in the U.S. Business travel will come back, even if it doesn't rebound to pre-Covid levels, and if this is part of your career and you want to still have time with your family or spouse, you need to learn the nitty-gritty. Efficiency is everything. This is timeless!

First of all, you need to achieve airline status. Sign up for miles programs with all the airlines you fly most often, then shoot for the highest-class miles status you can achieve, whether it's called Gold, Platinum or Extra Super-Duper Platinum. (Note: However high your status, airlines can always create a new class with higher miles requirements.) Looking back at our total lifetime miles accumulated over decades, we realized Ilene gathered some 4.5 million miles and Bram some 9 million—counting just Bram's miles, that's roughly 18 round trips to the moon. Not only does miles status get you upgrade consideration, but if your flight gets canceled, airlines will tend to your needs ahead of those with lower status. (And over the years, we used a lot of those miles to pay for vacation flights with the kids.)

In the U.S. before 2020, business travelers made up 12 percent of airline passengers, but they generated from 24 to 75 percent of airline earnings per flight,[64] and they booked an estimated 445 million business trips per year.[65] Of course, we ended up traveling a lot more than a typical businessperson who travels only occasionally. Aside from careers in the travel industry itself (airline pilot, hospitality industry), the top careers requiring frequent travel include management consultant—like Bram—event manager, public accountant or auditor, public or media relations, and regional sales representative.[66]

You should also familiarize yourself with the airlines and routes you usually fly, as well as key airports along the way where you might need to change planes—although nonstop flights are always preferable. Most of this you can research in advance, but some things, like familiarity with specific airports, you may have to learn through experience. On long flights, try to book an airline with lie-flat beds so you can actually sleep. If you must change planes, you should know at what times of day that airport has flights—and how many—to your destination. If something goes wrong, familiarity with flights and routes can make the difference between being stuck for an extra hour or an extra day. Sometimes, for instance, it can make sense to book a flight through Hong Kong versus Singapore or even Tokyo for just this reason.

And, of course, if you do any international travel, you should apply for Global Entry. It really eases your way through passport control.

Many people imagine all this travel must be overwhelming or oppressive in some way, but we've always seen it as a positive, not a negative. A long flight, especially, can be a chance to rest and regroup. For Bram in particular, travel was pretty much the entire game, and mastering all the variables involved did have a game-like quality. The ideal was to arrive at your destination as quickly and efficiently as possible, and the least tired. If you managed to get five hours of sleep in a lie-flat bed on an overnight flight, arriving well-rested enough to attend a morning meeting, you had done well.

Obviously, if we hadn't been required to do quite as much travel, that would have been better, but there was no other way to do our jobs, so we tried to make the experience as positive as we could. We couldn't really imagine zero travel, and we still enjoy traveling to this day.

Sometimes this mastery of the variables paid off on a personal level. When Bram was working in South Africa, he got word that his father had died. He managed to catch a flight out of Johannesburg that night, got to JFK by 6am, and arrived home in Paterson, New Jersey, before noon, ahead of his sister, who traveled up from Thomasville, Georgia.

We developed several specific, practical rules for ourselves to help us move fast and stay rested. We never checked luggage, just traveled with a carry-on. Ilene would always pack an exclusively black and white wardrobe, so everything matched. Bram would always get his shirts from the dry cleaner folded, with medium starch, to minimize creases when he unpacked. If he ever got stuck for an extra day in Detroit, say, he'd just buy new socks and underwear at Walmart. We never drank alcohol while flying, even if it was free, and ate lightly.

We preferred to travel alone versus with colleagues because you could be more productive and/or get more rest, but we couldn't always control this. If it was a three-hour flight with colleagues, you were expected to chat about business the whole flight. On an eight-hour flight, it was fine to chat for an hour and then start reviewing business-related materials or try to doze off. Generally, you'd prepare for your upcoming meeting or assignment on the flight out, then relax a bit on the flight back—maybe watch a movie, get some sleep or, in Ilene's case, pay some bills. When Bram was commuting on the short, early flight to Detroit, often with colleagues, he developed the skill of dozing off at takeoff for an extra 30 minutes of sleep.

When traveling alone, be careful if you want to be left alone. Never say hello to the person next to you unless they greet you first. In that case, be polite but not overly engaging. Don't give them an opening to a conversation you don't want to have. After brief pleasantries, put on some headphones and open a laptop, a book or a folder full of dense documents—or pretend to fall asleep.

You should also know your own biorhythms and try to schedule things to work with them when possible, especially because you may be jet-lagged much of the time. For instance, Bram is a morning person. So, getting up at 5am for a 7am flight was no problem for him.

Ilene is not a morning person, and she worried about the unpredictable morning traffic: When she had to make an early flight, she would spend the previous night at an airport hotel and just walk over to the terminal. The cost of the hotel (reimbursed by her employer, of course) was worth it for more rest and less worry.

And we would discuss any long flight before either of us booked it. One of us would say, "Let's review the rules for Europe and Asia," and we'd refresh our minds with relevant rules of thumb. We'd also update them, passing on any new tips about specific airports, say, that one of us had learned, always expanding our pool of knowledge.

LESSONS:

• **If you do much business travel, learn the nuts-and-bolts details in terms of airports, routes and airlines. Efficiency is everything.**

• **Use the rules you create to minimize stress and simplify decisions.**

• **If you travel for business, attain airline status via miles—the higher the status, the better.**

• **Apply for Global Entry (or the post-pandemic equivalent) if you travel internationally.**

• **When flying, pack lightly, eat lightly and do not drink alcohol.**

• **Avoid checking your bag. Checking luggage adds precious minutes to your trip and can separate you from your colleagues.**

• **On long flights, try to limit conversation with colleagues and strangers so that you're free to work, relax or sleep.**

CHAPTER 6

Managing Money

We realize that we've been fortunate in being able to reach retirement with some money to spare. Not many career paths, even medicine or law, offer the same earnings opportunities as a career in management consultancy or the rewards of being a successful CEO of a large company. But we didn't start out with money, and many of the fundamentals of managing family finances—like harmonizing attitudes toward spending and saving—apply broadly to many couples.

We both grew up with a sense of frugality, for somewhat different reasons. Ilene's family didn't have a lot of money, but she grew up in a town where many people had more. These people weren't radically different from Ilene and her family in other ways, they were just a bit more prosperous. They belonged to country clubs and vacationed in Florida. To Ilene, they seemed to be leading fun lives, and she wanted to have fun, too. Her mother would say to her, "We don't have that kind of money." Ilene's family was a typical middle-class one, but they used credit to keep up with the Joneses, which drove Ilene crazy. This reinforced her desire to earn more money than her parents.

Ilene worked at a series of jobs while going to school, including as a supermarket cashier. When she was 19, she took a trip to Europe, paid for with $800 she had saved up. When she first met Bram, she was working at the Boston Consulting Group with two degrees from MIT, but she was saddled with student loans, giving her a negative net worth.

This experience instilled in her a desire to be successful and make enough money to have the freedom to enjoy her life without worrying about it. She considers herself lucky not to have grown up on top of the heap, among the wealthiest families in her community. A little bit of envy lit a fire under her and gave her something to aspire to.

Bram grew up in a family that was a bit more comfortable financially than Ilene's. Bram's father taught him both how to budget and how to write checks: He gave Bram a checkbook to use to draw on his allowance. When Bram needed some money, he filled out a check—this had to be done correctly—and left it overnight on a side table. In the morning, the requested 10 or 25 cents would be there next to his check. His father would also oversee while Bram balanced his checkbook. His sister would spend her entire allowance quickly, but Bram liked the feeling of security it gave him to know he had 25 cents still in the "bank."

Bram also developed an entrepreneurial streak, selling tomatoes grown by his grandfather out of a wagon or shoveling snow for neighbors. He would buy a box of 24 chocolate bars, then sell the treats individually around the neighborhood at Halloween time, making a profit of 10 or 20 cents per box.

When Ilene first got hired by BCG, she suddenly found herself earning $25,000 a year. This was in the mid-1970s, when the median U.S. household income was around $13,000, according to the U.S. Census Bureau. "Oh my god," she thought, "that's so much money!" Ilene realized she was earning close to what her father, an independent CPA, was earning after working for decades.

Consulting firms always had a reputation for paying well. Newly minted MBAs and senior partners (not including awards of stock or stock options that may be granted to partners) have a pay differential that's relatively narrow, no more than a factor of four or five. Including base pay and performance bonus, a freshly hired MBA earned as much as $210,000 in 2019, while a senior partner—a position someone might attain after a decade at a consulting firm—earned as much as a million bucks.[67]

Within a couple of years of Ilene's hiring, the two of us were living together in London, and we started to notice a divergence in our attitudes toward spending. It wasn't anything drastic—neither one of us wanted to spend everything we were earning. But Ilene was in more of a hurry than Bram to upgrade their lifestyle as soon as they could. Her natural inclination was to spend maybe 10 percent more than Bram would have. Luckily, Bram didn't really mind being prodded in this direction. He came to realize that he might be a little too conservative on this front and that, whenever Ilene convinced him to spend a bit more, he found himself enjoying it in one way or another.

For instance, Bram would usually do the food shopping, and in London he would go to Safeway to buy groceries. But in the late 1970s, meat in London was slightly better than leather. At one point we discussed the possibility of buying steaks from Harrods, but Bram dismissed the notion: "We don't need steaks from Harrods." So, one day Ilene suggested steaks for dinner and even offered to pick them up. She brought home one steak from Safeway and one from Harrods. After that, Bram caved. He wasn't about to eat shoe leather while he watched Ilene devour prime beef from the grasslands of Ireland.

> **LESSON: Be self-aware and honest with yourself about your attitudes toward money, and be sensitive to your partner's attitudes. It's rare for both partners to hold exactly the same attitudes, so how you will spend money—as individuals and as a couple—should be openly negotiated. Leaving differences or tensions in your approach to money unacknowledged is a recipe for trouble in the long run.**

Despite these slight differences, we both grew up with pretty similar values. Certain things we both refused to skimp on, starting with anything that affected our children's well-being and, thus, the nanny. We both supported spending what was necessary to live our lifestyle. And over time our attitudes converged, so Bram loosened up about spending and Ilene became more of a saver until we met in the middle. (The average American household saves about 9 percent of after-tax income per year).[68]

We liked to take great vacations in the Caribbean, but we'd try to be as frugal about it as we could. Once Emily was born, the three of us would stay in one room rather than a suite. With Andrew along too, we'd book two connecting rooms, boys and girls. Sometimes we'd book rooms on a higher-cost floor so we'd get free breakfast. And we'd use airline miles to save on our vacations any way we could.

To this day, Ilene manages airline miles to maximize their value. When renting a car, she'll check four or five different rates before deciding on one. And she still gets excited about sales at Bloomingdale's.

So, we always saved as much of our income as we could and gradually built wealth. Some people make a lot of money and buy fancy boats or airplanes or multiple houses scattered around the world. None of that made sense to us or held much appeal, so we avoided big, flashy purchases.

We both liked the feeling of having some money for the sense of security and relative freedom it provided, but we never deliberately set out to accumulate as much money as we could. We were competitive, achievement-oriented people. Every raise or bonus or award of stock options felt like a recognition of our accomplishments. It's how we knew we were performing well.

Success is about adding value in some way and following your passion. Always look for an organization and a job where your abilities, intelligence, skills and experience can add real value. If you add enough value, you'll be rewarded. If your primary passions are your work and your family, you may be suited to adopt our model for success.

If you have no passions and just want to punch a clock, this book is not for you.

But we weren't competitive with each other, because we operated as a true partnership. (We pooled our assets and maintained joint bank accounts.)

During most of our careers, Bram earned more than Ilene. It was only during the last eight years of Ilene's career, when she became CEO of Ingredion, that she earned more than Bram, as the bulk of her compensation came in the form of awards of equity in the company. Bram didn't mind that she was earning more. His attitude was, "Great—more for us!"

And as a CEO, Ilene developed a higher public profile—she became more famous than Bram. But Bram, who had been very well compensated for years, felt secure in his accomplishment.

LESSONS:

• **You must be true partners in this enterprise to make it succeed. Both of you are presumably driven to achieve at work and pulling your weight within the family. So, there's no point in competing with each other on earnings or anything else—this should be the two of you against the world.**

• **Saving as much as you can is a slow but steady way to build wealth.**

• **Success is about adding value and following your passion.**

Our single best investment was investing in each other and making each other successful. Some of this investment was financial, especially in the early years when we had young children, to pay for a nanny and whatever other support we needed. And when you're spending money to make it all work, there may not be a lot left over from one of the salaries. But this is a long-term investment that will allow both partners to maximize their earnings over time. In the long run, it can pay for itself many times over.

But much of this investment was emotional and thoughtful, a matter of providing advice, encouragement and support—both privately and publicly—and being honest and flexible with each other in working around any bumps in the road. In a dual-career household, emotional success is really as important as financial success.

None of our investments in real estate over the years were very consequential—we didn't regret any of them, but none of them led to huge windfalls. When private equity deals became popular around the early 1990s, we dipped a toe into a few of those. None of those deals paid off, but we never gambled more money than we were comfortable risking.

But for the most part, we outsourced investing to our financial advisor. (Only some 17 percent of Americans use a financial advisor, according to an April 2019 survey by CNBC and Acorns.[69]) In the 1980s Bram was working at consulting firm Booz Allen, and they offered all sorts of benefits designed to take care of aspects of employees' personal lives so the employees could stay focused on work. So, that got us started with a financial advisor we really liked, and we've stayed with him for 45 years, following him after he left to start his own practice. He's smart and open, and he realized from the start that he had two clients on his hands, not one. This is really the case with any couple, but especially so with dual careers.

We have complementary investment styles. rather than overlapping investments. So, we meet with our advisor every quarter and have a smart conversation, and he listens to both of our viewpoints. He provides all sorts of services besides investment strategy: estate planning, cash management, tax planning. These are all chores that need to be done, like grocery shopping, so we outsourced them. He's become like a family CFO.

LESSONS:

• **Our single best investment was investing in each other—both financially and emotionally—and making each other successful.**

• **Delegate to a financial advisor. Make sure to find one who truly listens to both of you and doesn't simply impose his own preferences. The advisor must treat you as a dual-career couple and be mindful that he has two clients.**

Photographs

Bram, circa 1976: adventurous, unattached—and dispatched to South Africa at age 28 by The Boston Consulting Group (BCG), early in his consulting career.

Right: Ilene in the late 1970s. While Bram was in South Africa, she navigated her first year or so as a consultant with great success, even though she often felt like a geeky outsider.

Below: The nameplate Ilene demanded to replace "Miss Gordon."

MS. GORDON

Bram officially proposed to
Ilene on Valentine's Day
1979, but because BCG
needed them to open up its
Chicago office, they were
determined to plan and
pull off their wedding in
two months. "I didn't
have time to spend a year
on engagement parties,"
Ilene explains.

Saturday night, April 21, 1979, Copley Hotel, Boston: the
wedding. The very next day, Bram and Ilene flew to Chicago,
arriving on Sunday night, and were the first two employees at
the BCG office on Monday morning.

ILENE GORDON AND BRAM BLUESTEIN

"Tied together," in this case by similar corporate neckwear. By June 1981, Ilene was part of corporate America, working for Signode Packaging.

Bram functioned as the official photographer for his family's spring getaway to Disney World in 1988. Vacations were always given priority to maintain a healthy work-life balance. Here, Ilene holds fast to the couple's most precious assets: Emily and Andrew.

A dual-career family has to make choices: Attending Ilene's brother's 1988 wedding in Boston was a no-brainer for the Chicago-based family. Left to right: Andrew, Bram, Emily, Ilene.

Happily doing "Daddy duty." Early on, that meant fun in the sun and sand of Caribbean vacations like this one at Club Med in Eleuthera, 1991. Today, it means regularly teeing up together on the golf course or bundling up to cheer on the Chicago Bears.

Emily's bat mitzvah, October 1994, Winnetka, Illinois. Ilene recalls, "I invited female leaders— all two of them— from work. Counting me, there were three women in leadership roles in an office of about 100 staffers."

Family summer fun pre-college—this time, in Europe. This was Andrew's first trip abroad. We wanted to show our children the world. Here we are at dinner in Positano, Italy. We also visited London, Paris and Rome.

Ilene and Bram were at the top of the world—the corporate world, that is—at the World Economic Forum in Davos, Switzerland, January 2013. "Thanks to the time difference, at 11am in Switzerland I got to ring the New York Stock Exchange's 4pm closing bell," Ilene says.
Here, the couple rubs elbows with the financial journalist and news anchor Maria Bartiromo.

July 2018: On Ilene's retirement, Ingredion created the Ilene Gordon Scholarship for high school girls interested in STEM (Science, Technology, Engineering and Mathematics). The funds benefit Girls 4 Science, a grass-roots organization founded to fuel the interest of 10- to 18-year-old girls in Chicago in STEM education. Here, Ilene and the first two recipients proudly display the awards plaque.

Validation from on high: In October 2019, The Wall Street Journal *invited Ilene and Bram to speak about their household's ground rules—what the couple terms their "secret sauce" for a successful dual-career family—at its Women in the Workplace conference in San Francisco. Here, Karen Pensiero, managing editor of the WSJ, interviews them.*
Credit: ProductionManager.com/The Wall Street Journal/Andy Davis

Portrait of a thriving dual-career family, September 2021: (l to r) Andrew Bluestein now heads his own investment firm, Bluestein Ventures. Emily Bluestein is a principal in BEA Real Estate Enterprises LLC. Today, both of them tip their metaphorical hats to Ilene and Bram for being such loving parents, such valuable mentors and such deeply treasured friends.

CHAPTER 7

Making Inevitable Tradeoffs

Everyone makes tradeoffs in life, but for dual-career couples, these may be especially sharply defined. Still, they do not need to be particularly painful. Tradeoffs are simply choices you make, and as long as your priorities are clear, the choices are rarely difficult.

For both of us, our twin priorities and passions were career and family, so it was natural to let other activities fall by the wayside. When we were a young couple without children, we certainly didn't feel constrained. We had two incomes and satisfying careers. In our free time, we were doing exactly what we wanted. It never occurred to us that we couldn't "have it all."

But the arrival of children changes the equation and focuses the mind—despite the chronic lack of sleep entailed in the first months of parenthood. Being responsible for children, especially young ones, aside from being devoted to a demanding career, is quite a juggling act in itself. There's no way to manage it without organization, self-discipline and a good support system. And a second child just increases the time demands and complexity exponentially.

Luckily, organization and discipline are among Ilene's strong points. She very much wanted a family and really enjoyed her career, but she didn't much mind giving up other things. She had never been an athlete, and she found rewarding intellectual challenges at work. We didn't throw dinner parties, and we didn't have a lot of time to go out with friends, but a limited social life seemed like a reasonable tradeoff.

To Ilene, looking back at what she gave up, her biggest regrets are not having more time sitting on a beach reading novels—virtually the only time she allowed herself the indulgence of fiction—and not getting more sleep. She always tried to get in seven hours a night but didn't always succeed. (According to the National Sleep Foundation, the average healthy adult needs seven to nine hours.[70])

The real tradeoffs, for Ilene as for so many women, were not about disappointment at missing out on fun activities or the freedom of more time. They were about guilt at the thought that she might have fallen short of an idealized standard of the perfect mother.

Mulling this over, we realized that there's a significant gender gap when it comes to tradeoffs. Career women with families, too often told they can have it all, attempt the impossible and find themselves painfully stretched between the poles of family and work, constantly fretting that they've neglected one or the other. We found that the ideal situation was to find the balance that enabled a successful career and a happy family.

Many men tend to see the tradeoffs they make through a different lens. As they become fathers and face new time constraints, they realize they'll have to give up some "guy stuff," or at least do it much less often. That weekly pickup basketball game or poker night, those weekend fishing trips with the guys, all may have to be put on indefinite hold, at least until the kids are much older.

Men who give up such things for the sake of more family time may feel some disappointment at the loss or twinges of regret at the vanished freedom of their youth, but they're not usually racked with guilt. They may even get a pat on the back for their "maturity." And since they're giving something up for a worthy cause, they can feel good about themselves. But women are simply expected to devote themselves to the kids, and whenever they suspect they might be falling short of the standard their own mothers set, they beat themselves up for it.

Ilene's mother told her she wasn't ready to be a mother simply because Ilene wasn't willing to give up her career. Such expectations are internalized by women and weigh on them. The reality, studies have shown, is that stay-at-home moms spend about the same amount of time with their kids as working moms, because stay-at-home moms take up other activities, such as charity work, hobbies or socializing. And a 2012 Gallup poll of some 60,000 women found that stay-at-home mothers are more likely to report feeling sadness or anger than working mothers.[71]

For Bram, the tradeoffs were fairly straightforward. He played a lot of tennis in his youth but eventually gave it up for lack of time. He didn't take up golf—a very time-intensive game—until later in life, because his son got interested in golf. He gave up time working out in the gym, and he never got together with the guys to watch Monday Night Football. But none of these tradeoffs were terribly difficult for Bram. While it would have been nice to have a bit more time for himself and leisure pursuits, he was pretty content with the way his life was structured: work during the week, Saturday nights with Ilene, and the rest of the weekend for family time with the kids.

The bottom line: We worked hard, played hard and vacationed even harder. You might say we vacationed systematically. This usually involved a beach in Florida or the Caribbean and stacks of books that we bought to bring along—fiction for Ilene, nonfiction for Bram. At the end, we would tally up the number of books we read as a measure of the vacation's success. (Admittedly, we may be a little obsessive about measuring success.)

Of course, we both shared a limited social life. Our friends basically self-selected—those who understood our lifestyle, didn't judge us and didn't expect us to be available all the time. We had very good friends who we might go out to dinner with two or three times a year to catch up. They didn't demand to see us more regularly.

Ilene acknowledges missing the sort of deep friendships with other women she experienced in high school and college. She had no time to cultivate those—and such close bonds are more difficult to establish in adulthood for most people.

But she really enjoys meeting people she classifies as "interesting," and she keeps an eye out for them. These tend to be people who have overcome major challenges in life or have been pioneers in some way. People who lost their parents at a young age and worked three jobs to get through school. In corporate life, these were the sort of people she liked to hire. People who grew up privileged and went straight to Wall Street were "boring."

Overall, we're both content with the choices we made and satisfied with the lives we've led so far.

Part of the key here is deciding which pursuits are relatively low priorities for you and can be surrendered without too much pain. Try to hang on to those things that give you a lot of satisfaction. It helps to select a hobby that you can engage with in brief chunks of time.

LESSON: Both members of any dual-career couple with children need to clarify their priorities and choose how to use their time. You certainly need to prioritize family and work. Career demands can be all-consuming. You will need to make tradeoffs, but the precise choices are yours. Both members of the couple should focus on minimizing their disappointment, set aside unproductive guilt, and spend as much time with their kids as they can.

Obviously, some of the choices we made might not suit everyone. You have to sort out your own priorities. And some highly successful people have followed different paths.

For instance, CEOs of large companies who somehow carve out the time to maintain strong involvement in hobbies, sports or other passions certainly exist. A handful of studies have examined how various pursuits correlate with their job results.

Harvard Business Review took an interesting look at this recently.[72] The researchers examined public information on the CEOs of S&P 500 companies and found 56 who had a "strong leisure interest." They then pored over thousands of articles, social media posts and videos to form a detailed picture of their pursuits and interviewed 17 of these CEOs.

These various passions are often something these CEOs took up in their youth and have stuck with ever since. The researchers wanted to "investigate *why* leaders make time for passionate leisure interests in their already impossibly busy schedules—and whether they feel it helps their job performance."

(One thing to note: This comprises only some 10 percent of S&P 500 CEOs. So, they are more the exception than the rule.)

The CEOs themselves clearly feel their hobbies help them cope with the stresses of their job. Many of them block off time for their interests far in advance to protect those interests from being eaten up by other demands. *HBR* also points out that, on average, CEOs have a total of 2.1 hours of downtime a day—reading for pleasure, watching TV, hobbies—and that time is fragmented.[73] Carving out the time for a serious passion is no mean feat. So, how are these activities helpful?

One key way: Many of these CEOs have hobbies that demand total immersion, thus refreshing their brains from thinking about work. During most other downtime activities, whether they're having dinner with the family or watching TV, work issues continue to churn in the back of their minds. They deal with so many pressing problems that it is hard to turn off work. But when you're sparring with someone in martial arts training (like Electronic Arts CEO Andy Wilson), playing a guitar with a band (like George Barrett, former chairman of Cardinal Health) or piloting a plane, you need to clear your head and focus intently on the moment.[74]

Another appeal: Many of these hobbies offer endless room for continual self-improvement. There are always new levels of mastery to attain or more competitions to win. They allow people to deploy a certain sort of obsessiveness on something other than work. This attracts many CEO types.

And some point out that—usefully—these pursuits can help keep you humble. You won't always be the fastest cyclist in the race or the best musician on stage. It can be refreshing to step away from the expectation that you always be "top dog."

Others say that their hobby clarifies their thinking, gives them energy or has taught them valuable lessons, from keeping cool in a crisis to picking their battles.

One other thing struck us as worthy of note: This sample of CEOs was almost entirely male, through no fault of the researchers. Only 30 of the S&P 500 CEOs are women, and only one woman was mentioned in the article: Nasdaq CEO Adena Friedman, who practices tae kwon do.

LESSON: If you're truly passionate about some pursuit that helps you deal with stress and makes you more

effective in other areas, feel free to try to keep it up. But don't pressure yourself to become a black belt or a concert pianist. Balancing career and family is tough enough on its own.

Another important consideration is that both spouses need to feel that the overall balance of tradeoffs is fair, but this is not something you want to micromanage. Trying to track every minute of your own downtime or your spouse's to impose some strict regimen is bound to cause friction and resentment. You need to trust each other to operate in good faith with the full intent to pull your weight for the family. You should be able to feel the balance intuitively.

Of course, from time to time something might come up that one of us wanted to spend extra time on and that needed to be negotiated between us. Such things were "discussable." Other things were not discussable, like Ilene's need for time to get her hair colored regularly. This never affected Bram anyway, since she somehow managed to get this done during the workweek—he had no idea how.

In fact, Ilene got her hair done by insisting on efficiency. She would find a salon that stayed open into the evening and eschew any fancy multiprocessing of her hair that would take a few hours. Ilene would show up after work, at 5:30 on a Thursday evening, and be on her way home by 7.

When time is your most precious resource, efficiency is a huge factor, and Ilene pursued it relentlessly. For example, she enjoyed shopping, but only if it was efficient. So, she cultivated a relationship with a saleswoman at a store that sold business apparel, becoming one of her best customers. The saleswoman got to know Ilene's taste, size, colors—black, white and blue—and, eventually, she knew what Ilene already had in her closet.

Twice a year, in March and August, Ilene would research the possibilities in advance, then call ahead to the store. She would arrive to find an array of relevant choices ready for her. So, she could leave work at 5, buy a whole season's wardrobe in an hour, and be home by 7.

In general, Ilene made a practice of trying to deal only with people who were fast, efficient and worked hours that were convenient for her. And while good grooming was important for professional reasons, Ilene was rather strict about what she allowed herself. For example, she considered pedicures reasonable because she could read while they were done, but manicures struck her as too much of a waste of time. She did her own nails late at night. For efficiency, Ilene made the effort to get things done during the week, as our nanny was available, and this made more time for parenting on the weekends.

Another way to boost efficiency is to make your time dual-purpose whenever possible, accomplishing two things at once. Whenever Ilene flew somewhere, she spent the time reading documents to prepare for a meeting, paying bills or sleeping. When Bram took the kids out for Saturday breakfast, he was both enjoying his time with the kids and letting Ilene sleep in.

Another dual-purpose example: Some years ago, we both attended a dinner at the Economic Club of Chicago—Bram was there as a consultant representing his firm, and Ilene was invited as a CEO representing her company. We both came from work and arrived separately, so no one realized we were married, even though we ended up seated at the same table. We didn't see any reason to clue everyone in—Bram wanted to give Ilene room to shine on her own. But we also couldn't resist flirting openly with each other through dinner, thus networking, having fun and strengthening our marriage all at once. Afterward, someone from our table saw us leaving together and remarked, "You're married? Thank God! I thought there was a scandal brewing."

Bram enjoys watching sports, but while the kids were growing up, he would never sit down and watch them on TV unless the kids were watching—in which case, they were spending time together, sharing interests and bonding, as well as enjoying the game. He never imposed his own interests but happily and spontaneously shared this one with the kids. The long-term result: Andrew is an avid Bears fan, and Emily is devoted to the Cubs. Now that Bram is "retired" and not working so intensely (see Chapter 10, *Rewiring*—Not Retiring), he's become "the biggest ticket broker in Chicago," with season tickets to both the Bears and the Cubs, a fun way to spend time with our now adult kids.

Besides being efficient, it's important to be opportunistic when seizing time for yourself. As the night owl in the family, Ilene grabbed her alone time while everyone else slept. But she wouldn't just watch TV. Often, she liked to unwind by planning something.

And when downtime naturally presents itself, embrace it and enjoy. For instance, Ilene always looked forward to the winter holiday season and threw herself into it, savoring the two-week lull and hanging out with the kids. It was precious time. But a two-month lull would have been way too much.

LESSONS:

• **You can't have it all—not at the same time, that is. But if you plan and schedule diligently, you can have enough of what matters to you. If you're not willing to live a highly organized life, the combination of dual careers and a family is probably not going to work. Focus on controlling the things you can control. You need to learn to roll with the punches that you cannot control and figure things out as you go.**

• **In both work and family life, focus on things that you're good at and that bring you happiness. Try to always be present in the moment, even when the moment is unpleasant, and everything else should work out.**

• **Be efficient. It both improves your experiences and makes it possible for you to accomplish more.**

CHAPTER 8

Embracing Technology

Technology—specifically, information and communications technology—has played an increasingly pervasive and critical role in business as well as in just about every aspect of life during our careers. This accelerating revolution helped make the life we chose possible and certainly helped the family stay increasingly connected, regardless of business travel around the world. In fact, we probably would not have been able to do it were it not for the advances in technology. We strongly suggest that any dual-career couple embrace technology for organization and communication. The key is to use technology to simplify your life, not to complicate it.

Imagine what the world would have been had technology stayed stagnant over the last 40 years! In the late 1970s, when Bram was working for BCG and still single, he spent a year in South Africa. There was no internet. Mail was snail mail, and airmail was written on special, thin paper to save weight and expense. Newspapers communicated with their foreign bureaus by telex. There were no cell phones. There were landline phones, of course, but international calls were extremely expensive, so much so that Bram made a total of three calls home during that year. He mostly communicated with his family via airmail.

Today, when you get off the plane in Johannesburg, you turn on your phone and immediately connect to the local internet network, with your telecom carrier capping the cost at $10 a day. You check your email and voicemail, then call or text your family to tell them you've landed. And you're sitting in Johannesburg, but it might as well be a suburb of Miami, because the voice and data communications are so clear and easy. Technology has completely shrunk the world.

Bram was always ready to adopt new technology, while Ilene was happy to wait until the testing was over. Bram's enthusiasm goes back to his early adulthood, when he spent many hours at Columbia Business School analyzing data on a computer to develop insights from his professors' research. He went on to design educational testing systems while in the U.S. Army. At BCG he built the first direct-profit profitability model for a food and beverage packaging plant. Bram even saw the potential of the internet and aggressively adopted voicemail, email and texting on portable cell phones.

Not that Ilene is any sort of tech laggard—in fact, she counts some 300 apps on her phone, which is rather a lot, although she estimates she probably uses only 20 of them regularly. The average person now has more than 80 apps on their phone,[75] but 89 percent of their time is spent on just 18 apps.[76]

> **LESSON: Technology's greatest impact over the past few decades has been outward: The globe has shrunk and become much more intertwined. This has made it easier to manage a dual-career lifestyle while maintaining critical relationships.**

We both believe couples should use tech to simplify their lives. However, we also believe that the rules for dual-career couples that we have described in previous chapters, while modified by technology, stay fundamentally valid. So don't use technology as a justification to get around them.

As a dual-career couple, good communication is the foundation of your success. As years went by, technology made communication easier and easier, and it helped us bond as a family. When Bram was on a business trip in the early 1980s—before cell phones—he got a message under the door of his hotel room that read: "Call home." When he did, Ilene told Bram that she was pregnant with Andrew. As the kids were growing up, cell phones made it easier to deal with family emergencies, such as when Emily had a bike accident or when Andrew needed an emergency appendectomy. (The first cell phone—the

Motorola DynaTAC 8000X, which was a car phone—was sold in March of 1984, for $3,995.[77])

Looking back, it's clear that we couldn't have lived the lives we did without all this technology. For instance, the Detroit airport was once notorious for serious weather delays. Before the aerospace industry developed autopilot-assisted landings, allowing pilots to touch down in bad weather, Bram couldn't have commuted to Detroit three times a week. Without cell phones, Ilene could never have helped the kids study for spelling tests from the back of a cab, and Bram couldn't have instituted his practice of calling ahead on his way home from the airport so as to "never walk into a cold house."

But we never used technology to substitute for our time together, and even as technology was making virtual togetherness easier and easier, we observed our rules about time together in real life. Having Sunday dinner together was one of our rules.

We made sure that the four of us were physically together around the dinner table on Sunday evening, and we still believe that this is the best thing for a family to do. Leave Zoom for the rest of the week and celebrate Sunday together as a family. (Of course, this presumes you have kids still living at home.) We would talk about the coming week, catch up on the kids' homework and activities, including business and family trips that were coming up. Then Ilene would create a to-do calendar for the week that would include everybody's tasks and activities. Ilene used to copy the kids' school materials before traveling in case they needed to consult with her about their homework. Today, you can just go to a website and find the syllabus with links to the assigned reading.

These days we maintain an electronic weekly family calendar, which gets constantly updated and which each of us checks daily, simplifying organization. And while there is no longer the kids' homework to keep track of, we still work with our son, Andrew, and his venture capital firm, and Emily, with her real estate firm, so it's important to stay coordinated for professional reasons.

We also believe that the point of being together for a Sunday dinner is to be 100 percent present and interact with one another, not with technology. Unfortunately, families spend half of their evening meal distracted by electronics, toys and tasks that take them physically or mentally away from the table, according to a recent study of 109 families' dinnertime routines by University of Illinois alumna Jaclyn Saltzman, who conducted the research while earning a doctorate in family studies.

The same research confirmed what we have always supported—that both parents need to be present and involved with the family members around them during dinner. "Our findings suggest that fathers play an important role in interacting with and engaging children at the table," Jaclyn Saltzman, lead author of a study on the subject, told *MedicalXpress*. "When dads are present for meals, young children spend significantly less time playing with toys and other objects. Likewise, moms spend more time engaging in responsive eating behaviors, such as encouraging preschoolers to eat healthy foods and allowing them to decide whether and how much to eat."[78]

Because the temptation to consume technology may be as strong as the temptation to taste the food, we also approve of the rule, when you go out to dinner, the first person to check their phone has to pay for the meal. This helps combat the imperative that makes the average American check their phone 80 times a day, or every 12 minutes—*while on vacation.*[79]

We also have had several rules about specific blocks of time that were devoted to family. As a reminder, our 48-Hour Rule meant that, despite our heavy travel schedules, both of us had to spend at least 48 hours at home over the weekend. And the Saturday-Night Rule meant a date night for us as a couple. Bram wondered whether with all the videoconferencing today and the possibility of virtual togetherness, it might be possible to make it a 36-hour rule, which would allow one of the parents to fly in on Saturday or fly out on Sunday night. "No way," said Ilene. So, in the end, technology did not change the fundamentals, because the 48-Hour Rule was predicated on spending quality time as a couple and as a family in real life, not online.

Similarly, we used to have a rule that we wouldn't work at home on weeknights until the children were in bed, around 9. This should apply to work calls, too. So, if the CEO calls you at 7pm, you may think, "Wow, I get to talk to the CEO." But you should politely say, "Our family has a household rule, no calls from 7 to 9. Is it okay if I call you back then? Or tomorrow?" Odds are good that the CEO will understand. Dual-career couples need to communicate in order to create—and enforce—rules like this.

The downside of all this technology-enabled connectedness, of course, is that it's hard to disconnect; so, work and life tend to blur together more than ever. In 2012, Forbes Insights and Gyro published a report, "The @Work State of Mind Project," which found that only 2 percent of business decision-makers never work nights or weekends. More than half (52 percent) receive business information around the clock, including weekends. Fifty-three percent step away from dinner to deal with business calls, according to the report, which was based on a survey of 543 decision-makers in the United States and Europe.[80] As the title of the report points out, work has become a state of mind and not something we do from 9 to 5 in one location.[81]

Yet the survey also proves that there is a certain etiquette to being always on. The majority of survey respondents (64 percent) said that they work with people during personal time when they feel it's necessary, but otherwise try to respect some boundaries. And then there are those kind souls (36 percent) who believe there are some personal situations when people should be simply left alone. Of course, that still means that almost two-thirds of respondents or 64 percent would send a work-related email or text during, say, a wedding or a funeral.

Since that study was published, the avenues of virtual collaboration have exploded to include texting, Zoom, Slack and Microsoft Teams, to name just a few. It is thus more important than ever to set limits and enforce rules in this area—dual-career couples need to know how to unplug. When your attention is divided between work and family, you are not doing a good job for either. Let your co-workers know when you regularly block out personal time, which may vary depending on your job and family situation.

LESSON: Use technology to enhance your family communications, not to substitute for the time you spend with your family and certainly not to distract from it. Carve out times to be 100-percent present—physically

and mentally—for your family. Weekends or Sunday dinners worked best for us.

It is enticing to think that with all the collaboration technologies and remote work, it no longer matters where you live as a dual-career couple, but we don't believe this to be the case, at least not for a majority of dual-career couples. Selecting the right city for both of you, so that both of you are close enough to your offices, is still important (see Chapter 2: Finding the Right City).

In 2019 (we will be talking about 2020 and the pandemic in a later chapter), more than 26 million Americans—about 16 percent of the total workforce—worked remotely at least part of the time, according to the Bureau of Labor Statistics.[82]

An article in *Monitor on Psychology* notes that "…remote work can benefit both employers and employees, experts say. Employers can hire geographically distributed talent and reduce overhead expenses, while employees can gain flexibility, save time, and reduce transportation and some child-care costs. But the impact of such arrangements on productivity, creativity and morale has been up for debate, primarily because working from home offers employees fewer opportunities to talk and network with their colleagues."[83]

This view is supported in an article published by the Society for Human Resource Management: "Phyllis Reagin, founder of At the Coach's Table, a leadership coaching company in Los Angeles, noted that it's human nature for people to want to feel like they belong to a group. Good managers create cohesiveness among employees who see and talk with one another every day, but it can be easy for the manager and others to view team members who work remotely as 'outside' the group. For instance, she noted, remote workers can't have side conversations before and after meetings or conduct quick updates with others in hallways. They can't just pop into someone's office to ask a question or relay a funny story."

"There is a real strain on developing and maintaining important relationships," Reagin said. "The lower visibility may result in being passed over for prime projects, promotions and a lowered chance of salary growth."[84]

People feed off one another's energy. Ilene, for instance, was always very keenly aware when riding the elevator to her office in the morning that her co-workers were observing what mood she was in. She always tried to project optimism, so that people would feel comfortable about approaching her with any issues.

As a consultant, Bram believes that the best relationships are created when you start with personal interaction and then move to a technology-enabled space. Business is a team sport, not an individual sport, and you have to find ways to have personal interactions in order to maintain that teamwork.

LESSON: Selecting the right city—which allows both of the partners in the dual-career couple to be close to the office and put in face time at work—still matters, despite the changes wrought by Covid-19 and all the collaboration technologies that enable remote work.

Creating our professional identities was important for our careers (see Chapter 3, Forging Separate Professional Identities at Work, but One Identity at Home), but, unlike today, it did not involve building an online personal brand. About a decade ago, just half of CEOs had information other than their name on their company's website. Since then, the field of personal executive branding has emerged as its own cottage industry. Much of that branding is technology-enabled, via social media. Executives tweet, write blogs, have Instagram accounts, engage in discussions on LinkedIn and use Vimeo to add to their personal visibility.

Way back in 2015, only 39 percent of Fortune 500 CEOs were on any social media platform. But by 2020, 62 percent were present on at least one social media platform. A huge majority (94 percent) were on LinkedIn, the top platform for CEOs.[85]

We approve of creating an executive brand that helps the company that you are working for. Research found that a full two-thirds of consumers say that their perceptions of CEOs affect their opinions of companies and the products they sell. Executives, too, recognize the importance of leadership reputation—they attribute nearly one-half of a company's reputation to the CEO's reputation. Without any doubt, executive leadership is critical to burnishing the overall reputation of organizations today, as some 60 percent of a company's market value is attributed to its reputation.[86]

While individual executive personal branding started back in 1997, with an article in *Fast Company* titled "The Brand Called You," we never spent any time on our own personal branding to use it to enhance our careers. That article, written by Tom Peters, said: "Regardless of age, regardless of position, regardless of the business we happen to be in, all of us need to understand the importance of branding. We are CEOs of our own companies: Me Inc. To be in business today, our most important job is to be head marketer for the brand called You."[87]

That's not how we approached work. Ilene always focused on adding value to the business she worked for, and she was an active networker. This has earned her the best possible online presence, created by third parties, such as corporate listings, business magazines and industry associations, which are more credible than creating one's own story.

She has curated her professional identity over the years carefully, starting with using her own name early on, and always staying consistent on the message. She has also been consistent about her image. When she threw out the first pitch for the Chicago Cubs as the CEO of Ingredion, she wore an Ingredion jacket and a Chicago Cubs T-shirt.

Bram's online brand was part of the brands of the companies he worked for, which is still true today. He's co-founder, with his son, of Bluestein Ventures, a venture capital firm that invests in technology up and down the food supply chain. It has invested in companies that monitor trucks on the road and predict arrival times, as well as in restaurant technology to deal with the explosion of delivery services. So Bram, still keeping an eye on where tech is headed, is part of an online—and real-life—brand of Team Blue. Bram's bio on the company website, next to a blue-toned photo of Bram, explains that "his love for the food industry goes way back to his grandfather's butcher shop."

LESSON: Be deliberate and focused about creating your professional identity in real life, and create a consistent

version of yourself online. While the internet gives us all an opportunity to toot our own horns, it's always more credible if the praise comes from a third party.

Your technology usage probably reflects your own personality in some ways, and we're both used to planning, with an emphasis on effectiveness and efficiency, so this naturally imposes a certain discipline. Part of the key is to always bear in mind the fundamental objectives you're trying to accomplish: You want to communicate, coordinate, maintain a schedule. Stay focused on the goal, don't be driven by the tech itself.

Neither of us has ever developed a problem with obsessive tech use, but clearly many people do. A number of tech blogs, ironically, offer advice on how to control your tech use and keep it productive, especially in this era when so many are working from home. Naturally enough, they tend to advocate fighting fire with fire—using apps to control your usage.

Here's some typical advice:[88] Use an app such as Cold Turkey to limit the time you spend on social media or browsing for news during your workday, and an app like FocusMe to turn off distractions from all your devices. Use project management and collaboration tools (Trello, Evernote, Google Drive) to organize, collaborate and sync files on any device from anywhere. Use wellness apps to keep you from sitting all day, or an app like Headspace to take meditation breaks to reduce stress. Use workflow automation software to facilitate and control complex tasks—this integrates well with software such as Slack, QuickBooks and Google Docs.

Full disclosure: Neither of us has ever felt the need to adopt these tactics, so we can't personally vouch for their effectiveness. But if any of this advice resonates with you and your situation, it makes sense to give it a try.

LESSON: At some point, you have to manage the technology so it doesn't manage you. Stay focused on the goal: Do not be driven by the tech itself. If your tech use is becoming a time sink rather than a productivity

enhancer, try apps designed to help you control your use and to save you time and effort.

These days, Bram has started using Alexa, which he finds intriguing but still rather rudimentary. He's trying to get Alexa to control the Nest thermostat. And during the pandemic, we've been using an app called Caribou that lets us read books to the grandkids and play games with them. He's also started using an Owl (a new Zoom tool) to improve video calls.

Sometimes people ask us our opinions about pursuing a career in the tech industry. Our response: If that appeals to you, sure, why not? But the real key for careers isn't tech versus non-tech, it's simply high-growth opportunities versus everything else. For instance, consulting has been in a very high growth phase for the past 20 or 30 years, and that worked out quite well for Bram. But make sure you're involved in the core competency of the institution. In consulting, you could be on the client-service side. In tech, you'd better have some serious technical chops that will make you useful in product development or innovative marketing.

LESSONS:

• **Dual-career couples should embrace technology to organize their lives and communicate with their families. A family calendar can be very useful for this.**

• **Just remember to always focus on the ultimate goal, rather than let yourself be driven by the technology.**

• **Get involved in the core competency of a high-growth field if you can. This is the pathway to create the most opportunity.**

Weathering the Covid Stress Test—the Hybrid Workplace and the Post-Pandemic Aftermath

The pandemic of 2020 has completely upended the lives of dual-career couples, becoming a stress test of their resilience. It has added a new level of difficulty, requiring many parents to help educate and entertain their kids while performing demanding jobs from home. We believe that to weather this unprecedented period—and emerge stronger on the other side—dual-career couples need to be more inventive than they have ever been and work as a team.

Being a dual-career couple with a family is always a challenge, which is why we developed our rules and resolved to stick with them. Our framework of rules about family time—Sunday night dinners together, Saturday night dates—stays intact during the pandemic. We wouldn't adapt them for the pandemic—Covid cannot get in the way of being a family. (Admittedly, some rules, such as weekends at home or the 48-Hour Rule, may be superfluous for the duration of the pandemic since business travel has collapsed.) Other lifelong lessons such as being the right partner, establishing clear professional identities and building an infrastructure that allows both careers to thrive also continue to apply. These are the strong foundations that should help couples navigate this crisis-ridden time.

The biggest change would be about work-life balance during the pandemic. Dual-career couples typically have to contend with too little time to spend at home with each other and the family due to too much work and frequent travel. The pandemic reversed the equation. While it of course depends on the type of work, many dual-career couples and their families have had to deal with too much time together. As the parents worked remotely at home, their children were often out of school, also at home and in need of care and supervision.

In fact, given that we've both "rewired" (see Chapter 10, *Rewiring—Not Retiring*), the limitations on travel and the fact that, like so many, we've been spending time at home in our pod, the two of us have probably spent more time together in the past year than in the previous 40 years combined.

The need for reassessment of the roles and duties of the partners in a dual-career couple became painfully clear very early on in the pandemic, as the women in dual-career couples have been disproportionately punished by Covid-19. "Seven months into a pandemic that has turned work and home life upside down, working women are confronting painful choices that threaten to unravel recent advances in gender equity—in pay, the professional ranks and in attaining leadership positions," according to *The Wall Street Journal*.

"More women—particularly mothers—say they may have to step back or away from jobs they still have, a new major study shows. Though the pandemic has forced fathers and mothers to juggle careers with childcare and remote schooling, women often shoulder the brunt of those responsibilities."[89]

Research conducted by McKinsey & Company and LeanIn.org reveals that 18 percent of working mothers are considering dropping out of the workforce, at least temporarily—compared with 11 percent of fathers. An additional 15 percent of mothers report they may dial back their careers, either by cutting their hours or switching to a less-demanding role. Among women with young children, the struggle is especially acute: 23 percent say they may take a leave of absence or quit altogether.[90]

Yet, for all the challenges they face, dual-career couples have a few factors in their favor. Both members of the couple tend to be determined, driven and organized. And husbands in such couples are usually forced to develop their emotional intelligence to a greater degree than they otherwise might. As long as couples remain aware of the choices they're making, they have a good chance of negotiating a workable, equitable solution.

> **LESSON: The pandemic has become a stress test of the resilience of a dual-career couple, and made it plain that women are paying a higher price in terms of their careers. To weather this type of crisis, dual-career couples need to rely on a strong foundation as a family, while staying flexible and inventive about work rules.**

Take a thoughtful approach to reassessing work life during the pandemic. The actual crisis solutions are all tactical, and deal with scheduling, planning and delegating. But the overarching goal is to make both of you able to continue as an equitable dual-career couple. What we never want to happen is giving up because of misunderstanding or resentment due to lack of communication. To this end, have a thoughtful conversation and negotiation about your needs. If you don't have that initial conversation, what typically happens is that the woman fills the void, because that is the traditional behavior pattern. It's also often the path of least resistance, and it happens almost unconsciously.

That, in turn, leads women to feel guilt and resentment about not putting enough effort into their professional endeavors. One study found that, before the Covid-19 pandemic, there were no gender differences in self-rated work productivity and job satisfaction. However, during the lockdown, women reported lower work productivity and job satisfaction than men.[91]

We agree with an article in *Harvard Business Review* that states: "…the couples who survive crises with their relationship and careers intact are those who discuss and agree on certain principles as the crisis begins. These should capture what matters most to them, what they need and want to achieve, what they need from each other, and what they must give in return. It's these principles that, once set in an agreement, drive the practical solutions they adopt as the crisis unfolds."[92]

The devil, as they say, is in the details. In this case the hardest part is ironing out everyday schedules, even if you are both committed to the same goals. As we have explained in the parenting chapter, we were always very deliberate about planning and juggling the babysitting of our children, and it took organizational skills and inventive solutions to have all the time that we needed covered by a nanny. But we didn't have to factor in the Covid-19 virus.

What would we have done to assure that our children were being cared for during the pandemic so that both of us could have continued working? (Short answer: *Everything feasible!*) At the beginning of the pandemic, many parents did not want to have people from outside their immediate pod coming into their homes, which meant no childcare. At the same time, elderly grandparents who lived independently were no longer a backup plan either, since couples did not want to expose them to the virus. Even though we do not recommend grandparents as a long-term childcare solution, during the pandemic an already live-in grandparent would have been extremely helpful.

We admire dual-career couples who found ways to make it work. One couple we know, for example, split the day into two parts. One parent was responsible for childcare from 6am to 12pm, while the other one worked, and the schedule reversed from noon to 6pm. A study found that in dual-earning opposite-sex couples with young children, an "alternating day" strategy for childcare was associated with higher rates of individual well-being and job performance. A study of the childcare strategies for 274 dual-earner couples found that 37 percent used strategies where women did most or all childcare and 45 percent used egalitarian strategies. The model termed the "remote wife does it all" was associated with the lowest rates of well-being and job performance.[93]

After the initial hiatus, once Covid-19 testing became available, it came down to flexibility—on the part of the parents and the caregivers. For instance, you could change the typical nanny schedule of five days on and the weekend off, to 10 days on for the nanny, followed by four days off. This would allow ample time for testing before each ten-day stint.

Creating learning pods for your children with the children of a trusted, vaccinated friend or neighbor can be a useful strategy too. More parents can trade off on playing tutor, and the kids have friends they can socialize with.

LESSON: Adapt the work-life rules for the pandemic (and any other crisis). Be creative about scheduling. Keep things equitable, so all the childcare doesn't fall on one partner.

Like so many people, you may be feeling restless during the pandemic, experiencing some form of cabin fever, especially if you're used to frequent travel. In fact, this restless urge became so intense for some that certain airlines in Brunei, Japan, Taiwan and Australia (countries where Covid-19 was under relative control at the time) started offering—and filling up—short "flights to nowhere," landing at the same airport they took off from, with luxury service.[94] This may seem extreme, but some people missed the actual experience of flying that much.

A more productive response might be to make the most of this newfound time at home. Certainly, working from home is an adjustment, and it can be stressful, especially if you're stuck at home with restless kids. But this situation won't last forever. Seize the opportunity to strengthen your relationship with your spouse and to spend time with your kids. Open a bottle of wine and cook a lovely dinner together. Do things you never had time to do before. Learn to play chess or to play the guitar.

A study by *Forbes* and Zoom found that those with increased free time during the pandemic are using it for exercising (53 percent), cooking (50 percent) and spending time with family members (46 percent)—all of which contribute to better overall wellness. Another silver lining of the pandemic is that it has had a profound impact on all of us, not least by giving some of us more time to reflect on what's important.[95]

As a dual-career couple, you probably have had limited time for a social life anyway, but this no longer makes you odd. The playing field has been leveled in terms of social life, and you no longer have to feel guilty about not seeing friends or apologize for declining an invitation. Your family or your pod is now your social circle.

Another silver lining: If you're intrigued by the idea of working for a particular company that's based in a different city, this is a great time to get hired via Zoom interview with no pressure at all to show up in person, much less to relocate. The business world has completely adjusted to interacting virtually. (It's still helpful if the company isn't too many time zones away.)

In fact, McKinsey analyzed the potential of remote work in more than 2,000 tasks in 800 occupations across eight countries. The pandemic revealed that much more work could be done remotely and productively than business leaders previously believed, including "business sales calls, legal arbitration and trials, doctor visits, classroom learning, real estate tours, and even expert repairs of the world's most sophisticated machinery made with the help of virtual reality headsets."[96]

And this new, forced acceptance of virtual meetings and remote work will most likely result in permanent changes, with many companies adopting some sort of flexible hybrid model in terms of time in the office versus working from home—and leasing less office space. A McKinsey survey of executives in August 2020 found that they anticipate an average reduction in office space of 30 percent.[97]

Given the ascendance of remote work, if you haven't done it already, you should reassess your tech infrastructure at home (see Chapter 8, Embracing Technology). Make sure you have plenty of broadband capacity and that your devices and software are up to date. This is now your lifeline to both work and a virtual social life: Don't neglect it.

> **LESSON: Learn to embrace working from home and the boost in flexibility that set-up brings. Look for silver linings. Try to make the most of your increased time with the family—strengthen those bonds. And, whenever necessary, upgrade your technology.**

There have been other positive developments for dual-career couples that have spun off from the challenges of the pandemic. BCG lists four priorities for companies to support dual-career couples.[98] Just recently, all four were largely aspirational, but the pandemic has forced companies to implement big parts of three of these: Change the Support ("Use technology to enable flexible work"), Change How People Work ("Allow employees to work under flexible terms as long as their work gets done") and Change the Culture ("Reward results, not face time; reset working norms"). It's not clear that Covid-19 has had much impact on the fourth, Change What a Successful Career Path Looks Like.

In June 2020, the Center for Equity, Gender, and Leadership at UC Berkeley's Haas School of Business held a webinar/panel discussion on the impact of Covid-19 on dual-career couples, featuring executives from the consulting firm BCG, the customer-service software firm Zendesk, and the cloud-infrastructure and IT-security company Biarca.[99] Given the many stresses such couples are facing, mental health emerged as a key issue.

Brian Gross, North America Chief of Staff and West Coast Business Management Senior Director for BCG, noted that employees have become more open about mental health. BCG has been actively engaging with them, increasing flexibility of work hours, sharing techniques to improve work-life balance and clearing out Friday afternoon workloads.

Smita Pillai, Zendesk's VP, Global Head of Equity, Diversity and Inclusion, said that the company has introduced a new health app to give employees free assessments and health consultations, as well as flexible work hours. The firm is also encouraging time off for mental-health breaks and using a new pulse survey to check on stress levels and health.

And Subha Rajana, CEO of Biarca, added that, in addition to flexible hours and mental-health support, they are offering paid meals and introducing practices to reduce stress that employees can do at home.

Affinity groups or networks where dual-career couples can exchange tips and ideas, or just trade "war stories," are another good idea. Jill Zucker, a senior partner at McKinsey and part of a dual-career couple herself, felt there was a need for a way to have these sorts of conversations at the firm and to offer resources to couples. In 2017 she sent an email asking if anyone was interested in a dual-career couples' network. Even though this was on a Friday before a holiday, she received more than 100 responses in 45 minutes.[100]

We very strongly believe in being proactive, and we would thus advise creating dual-career couple affinity groups by yourselves. Think back to how Lamaze classes were helpful, how you felt that you and the other expectant parents were in it all together. Dual-career couples need to help each other and exchange ideas, the same way that women's networks assist women and parents' groups are there for parents. Let's carve out a niche for dual-career couples. If anything, the pandemic has revealed all the unmet needs of dual-career couples, and the need for their own support system. Let's create such networks, whether at the office, in your neighborhood or via Zoom.

LESSON: Take advantage of any useful programs or options your company has introduced. If it has an affinity group or network for dual-career couples, use it to garner practical tips and emotional support. If this doesn't exist at your company, consider lobbying to start one.

One factor that has changed during the pandemic is the dominance of major cities. In Chapter 2 (Finding the Right City), we stressed how important it is to live in a place where both careers can flourish. For the past decade, big cities in the U.S. and Europe have experienced the lion's share of job growth, while smaller cities have fallen behind, but remote work has rebalanced the equation. Whether this shift will prove permanent or temporary is unclear.

Now that no one is traveling for business and everyone meets by videoconference, secondary cities are much more competitive with major cities. It doesn't really matter if you're in the same city as your company. The real key is the culture of both city and company. Traditionally, people in big cities tend to be more open-minded, but some smaller cities will surprise you. The actual limiting factor for many dual-career couples in where they live is their kids and the reluctance to leave behind schools and friends. Of course, once business travel starts up again, large cities will regain a key advantage.

When tech companies shifted to remote work, many employees—faced with high rents, wildfires and a raging pandemic—fled Silicon Valley and the Bay Area.[101] While some sought refuge and the beach in San Diego, and others headed to major cities like New York and Chicago, the largest number moved to Austin, already a tech hub but a midsize city.

Office vacancy rates jumped in large cities in 2020, up 91 percent in San Francisco and 32 percent in London, while declining in cities like Charlotte and Glasgow.[102] Some smaller cities started incentive programs to encourage the trend: Tulsa, for one, offered relocating remote workers $10,000 and access to co-working spaces.[103]

McKinsey analyzed LinkedIn data and found that more members moved from large to smaller cities in 2020 than in 2019.[104] Major cities such as New York, San Francisco, Washington and Boston experienced the greatest outflow, while cities like Jacksonville, Salt Lake City and Madison, Wisconsin, had the biggest inflow.

Shifts like this could have unanticipated effects, some of them beneficial. If, say, a thousand dual-career couples move into a small or midsize city, this could change the culture, making dual careers seem more commonplace. These couples would be more likely to eventually meet one another, providing encouragement and comparing notes.

Post-pandemic, this trend could change again. Tax incentives or infrastructure improvements by cities could affect this.[105] Workers may reevaluate the pros and cons—the cost of living versus easy access to hubs for travel, opportunity and culture.

Another consequence of the widespread acceptance of remote work and videoconferencing will likely be a permanent decline in business travel. Leisure travel will probably bounce back after the pandemic due to pent-up demand, but McKinsey's travel practice estimates that 20 percent of business travel will not come back.[106] Some other estimates are even more dire, as high as 36 percent.[107] This can bode well for dual-career couples, who may be expected to spend less time on the road and end up having a better work-life balance.

LESSON: As long as the pandemic lingers, many dual-career couples have more freedom in where they choose to live, thanks to remote work and virtual meetings.

Some of this new geographic flexibility may well last beyond the crisis. Yet post-pandemic, it's quite possible that big cities will regain their luster.

CHAPTER 10

Rewiring—Not Retiring

Retirement is not what it used to be, certainly not the traditional idea many of us carry in our heads. Not many people still turn 65, collect a gold watch and a defined-benefit pension, then move somewhere warm to play golf or bridge and go on cruises for the next decade or so of life.

Our own approach to this stage of life is different enough from a traditional retirement that we adopted a more fitting term for it: "rewiring." (The term was coined by author Jeri Sedlar.) Given that successful dual-career couples naturally tend to have a strong commitment to their work, this approach may appeal to many of them.

To "rewire" rather than retire does not mean that you have to keep working for pay, even part-time, unless you want to work or need the extra income. You don't need to remain engaged with the business world, if that's where you come from—you could engage with the art world. You could write a book. Possibly for the first time in your life, you have the freedom to decide how to use your time: Rewiring is the process of reallocating that time. This means you can devote more time to your children and grandchildren—you're flexible. You might devote yourself to a non-profit organization, a political cause or a hobby that's a true passion for you. The key is to commit to staying active and engaged with the world as best you can.

LESSON: When you transition out of your full-time career, you don't have to devote yourself exclusively to golf, bridge or snoozing in a hammock—unless this

appeals to you. There are no hard-and-fast rules. You can choose to "rewire" in any number of ways, stay engaged, pursue something new—you can structure your time to do things you find deeply satisfying. Dual-career couples, who tend to be driven and organized, may find this especially appealing.

Bram is now entering his third phase of rewiring. In his first phase, he went to work for McNally Capital, a small private equity firm, as a senior advisor helping them do deals, develop people and define processes. In this phase, which lasted some five years, he was putting in a 40-hour workweek—a big step down from his previous 80-hour weeks.

In his second phase, Bram partnered with his son, Andrew, to help him test and launch his venture capital firm, Bluestein Ventures, which invests in visionary companies transforming the future of the food industry. Bram devotes a lot of time to that. Bram has also partnered with his daughter, Emily, in her real estate/property management business.

And now in phase three, after being rewired for 10 years, Bram is trying to manage down his commitments to the business world. He has pulled back from the venture business to become more a member of the investment committee and less of an active manager. He still spends considerable time discussing investment ideas with Andrew, but he's not tied to the office. He has withdrawn from a couple of non-profit boards and retired as a director of a for-profit company after 25 years.

Bram has been "filling his dance card" with other activities. "We've had a second home in Florida for some time," he explains, "but the 'pandemic winter' of 2020-21 is the first time we've spent the entire season in Florida." So, Bram has become a director of the condo association and found the time to play more golf—even during the week sometimes. And Bram and Ilene have both devoted time to writing this book.

Ilene, meanwhile, is still in phase one of rewiring. (Every time someone congratulated her on this new stage of life, she felt mildly annoyed. She'd think, "I'm not getting a pension, just Social Security and my personal savings—what are they congratulating me about?") She's doing a lot of board work, having recently taken on a third board at a for-profit company, and she's also involved with a non-profit organization. Her aim is to keep her commitments to about half her time, roughly 20 hours per week, but this is not steady—some weeks are busy and some are free. She's delighted to finally have time to read for pleasure, especially on the beach. She's also finding more time for golf, which means playing nine holes with Bram maybe once a week on average.

So, in phase one of rewiring, both Ilene and Bram dialed back their time commitments to about half their previous level—Bram was just starting from an initial level that was crazy high. The difference is simply one of preference and personality.

While you're pursuing a career full-time, you always have your foot on the accelerator, pushing as hard as you can. In our case, sometimes you push through the floor because you want to go faster. But somebody else actually decides how fast you go, whether it's the organization you're a part of or the clients you serve. Then you rewire, and suddenly, you really control the throttle. You control how you use your time and how much you want to work.

> **LESSON: When you rewire, you truly control your own pace and your own life, maybe for the first time ever. In phase one of rewiring, we both decided to cut our time commitments roughly in half compared to our previous full-time careers.**

One reason retirement is changing: People are living longer. In the U.S., a 65-year-old man can expect to live, on average, another 18 years, and a 65-year-old woman almost 21 years.[108] And that's just the average: So many people are living well into their 90s that planning for 30 years of retirement has become conventional financial advice. This longevity on its own is enough to reshape retirement.

Moreover, a lot of people still feel pretty vigorous at 65—or 75—and would like to remain engaged with the world. They want to use their experience to make a productive contribution. They don't want to be bored.

So our rewiring approach isn't utterly unique. You might even say we're part of a trend.

According to data from the Census Bureau and Bureau of Labor Statistics, analyzed by financial-planning firm United Income, as of February 2019 some 20 percent of those over age 65—10.8 million people—were working or looking for work.[109]

In fact, the percentage of 65- to 74-year-olds still participating in the labor force was 26.8 percent in 2016, and projected to reach 30.2 percent by 2026.[110] For those 75+, the figure is projected to reach 10.8 percent by 2026.

Understandably, working after retirement age tends to appeal to the well-educated in high-status jobs. In 2009, some 61 percent of those still working ages 62 to 74 had doctorates or professional degrees.[111] These white-collar jobs bring prestige. And these people like their careers. A 2013 AARP study found that 73 percent of the 60-to-74-year-olds cited job enjoyment as one of the most important reasons they still work.[112]

LESSON: More and more people continue to work at older ages, especially at high-status, white-collar jobs. This may appeal most to those least likely to really need the money. They do it to stay engaged, for prestige and because they enjoy the work.

Yet the practice we misleadingly think of as "traditional retirement" is itself a novel invention, going back only a few generations and largely limited to Westernized industrial societies. This sort of retirement involves a set retirement age (usually with some flexibility), and some kind of financial provision for retirees, whether state-sponsored, employer-subsidized or personal savings. Retirees are free to step away from productive work—and to some extent encouraged to, in order to make way for the next generation—with no stigma or loss of full status.

This approach is far from universal. A review of the ethnographic literature on retirement-like practices in non-Western societies shows an array of traditions.[113]

Among the Lusi of Papua New Guinea, old age is a relatively rare achievement, but the status of an elderly person depends on his or her independence, productivity and family relations. Traditionally, almost all illness and death are considered the result of witchcraft. The only "natural" or "good" death is that of someone who is dependent and decrepit. So, dependency becomes a kind of "social death."

In many societies, older people shift to less physically demanding tasks. For instance, among peasant societies in the Andes that survive by farming and herding, people work as long as they can do it physically. Older people transfer ownership of their fields to their children, but keep a separate home and a share of the harvest. They still herd, weed nearby fields, and shoo birds away from crops.

Another approach: The tradition among the Burmese is that the elderly refrain from economic activity and focus on religious duties. Financially supported by their families, they play important ceremonial roles, engage in good deeds and charitable works, and spend more time in meditation. This is considered a happy stage of life, with no economic burdens and no loss of status or influence.

In terms of retirement in America, various schemas of the phases have been proposed, ranging from three to six phases. Some focus on the progressive physical and/or financial limitations (the Go-Go, Slow-Go and No-Go phases[114]), others more on the emotional adjustments (Pre-retirement, Retirement, Contentment or Honeymoon phase, Disenchantment, Reorientation and Routine[115]).

We've refrained from developing an all-encompassing schema for rewiring with catchy names for the phases, because these stages will vary so widely depending on personal preferences and priorities. And while everyone goes through some sort of progressive easing of responsibilities, the number of stages may also vary. The details are impossible to predict.

LESSON: Different societies have evolved varied approaches to the elderly stage of life. If you live in the modern, Westernized world and are fortunate enough to

be fairly healthy and to have enough money, you have a good bit of flexibility. For the rewired, this stage of life is full of possibility.

While, of course, you should be saving for retirement over several decades, it's wise to take some time before rewiring to plan in more detail how you want to spend your time. We both feel that a year or so for planning is about right. For one thing, it can take some time to put the elements of rewiring in place.

The first obvious consideration is whether you really need, or want, to earn more income for some years in order to maintain the lifestyle you desire or for some other reason, such as beefing up what you plan to leave to your kids or grandkids. If so, that will constrain your choices and control your time. If this is not an issue, you're flexible.

But bear in mind, if you're rewiring, you're committing to more of a working lifestyle than a retirement lifestyle, especially in phase one. You won't be playing golf three times a week.

And you should be clear on the persona you're developing. For Bram, this meant developing a career as a private equity and venture capital investor. For Ilene, it was serving on corporate boards and making money.

So Bram's first phase of rewiring involved working at a private-equity firm and learning all he could. Ilene was already serving on two boards when she was a full-time CEO—which was crazy at the time, but it made for a simple transition. She just continued on those boards and later added a third. (She asked many people for advice: How many boards should I take on? A significant number advised: None, take a year off and then see how much time you want to commit. Other people say yes to everything—a difference in style.)

LESSON: Spend a year or so planning in detail for phase one of rewiring.

As we made the transition to being rewired, we also had to make two main adjustments. One was simply getting used to not having to show up at the office—something many people have had to adjust to during the pandemic, regardless of stage of life. The other was having to fend for ourselves regarding technology. Despite Bram's enthusiastic attitude toward tech and his early Mac infatuation, when you spend most of your time with your work laptop and work phone, you tend not to think about the nuts and bolts much. If there's an issue, you just call IT. It's surprising how much time it takes to master and maintain technology.

There are various types of this sort of office-dependence, which can intensify the minor shocks of rewiring or retiring. For instance, we've met many people who never make their own travel arrangements. Their flight gets canceled and they call the desk at global services, please get me on the next plane—which costs you time. We always had rules: Keep moving, go to the next flight, another airline, call the airlines ourselves. We were very self-motivated.

We've always wanted to keep learning all our lives, and that's one of the keys to rewiring. Stay engaged with the world, read the paper every day. If you're still connected to business, keep an eye on the stock market. Bram learned a lot about investing. Ilene needs to keep up with the industries related to her boards, whether defense, paper or food, and this comes naturally because she has a passion for these fields. You have to have passion for whatever you do. When you lose your passion, it's time to move on.

This raises the issue of how long members should remain on a board. Ilene questions why anyone would stick around for 20 years, which happens. Twelve to 15 years strikes her as a more reasonable maximum.

Then there's the question of boards of for-profit companies versus non-profits. Of course, one can serve on both types. While many non-profits are certainly worthy, Ilene prefers the for-profits. Partly this is because her boards keep her connected to industries she's familiar with and interested in. And partly it's because these are paid positions as opposed to most non-profit boards. This is not mainly a matter of the money per se but of the implied commitment. She feels people take paid positions more seriously.

LESSON: Never stop learning. If you're used to depending on corporate infrastructure, when you rewire you will have to learn to operate independently, which can be a

jarring transition for some. And if you lose your passion for what you're doing in this new phase of life, it's time to move on. Again.

And what about the larger question of the ideal age to retire—or rewire? Should there be a mandatory retirement age? We think the idea of forced milestones can be useful. We're not opposed to a mandatory age, but it should vary by profession. Some professors still deliver brilliant lectures at 80, but air traffic controllers face mandatory retirement at 56, with exceptions up to age 61.[116] In fact, consultants are often encouraged to retire at 60.

Many countries have a statutory retirement age at which people qualify for a full state pension or some equivalent (the details vary and are often complex). Most of these ages fall somewhere in the 60s, but they range from 55 (Sri Lanka) to 70 (Libya). In some countries the age for women is a few years lower than that for men. And the general tendency these days is for these official ages to gradually increase as the average lifespan grows.[117]

But it may be more revealing to look at what age people actually retire on average rather than the statutory age. A comparison based on Organisation for Economic Co-operation and Development data from 2013-18[118] shows this age at its lowest in South Africa (age 60), where the government does not impose an official age; so, workers negotiate this with their employer. The average retirement age climbs to 63.5 in Germany, 65.1 in Norway, 67.2 in the U.S., almost 70 in Japan and reaches a high of 72.3 in South Korea, 12 years higher than the official retirement age of 60. (South Korea has both long life expectancy and a high rate of poverty among elders, motivating people to work longer.)

We both love staying involved in the business world in some way, and many people over "retirement age" keep working in some capacity—full- or part-time, freelance, even volunteer—for the love of what they do. Others are happy to flee the working world as soon as they can, counting down the days to retirement and never looking back. Many of them engage with the world in other meaningful ways. We're not judging how anyone finds their bliss. This is about making choices when you're lucky enough to have them.

When and how you move from one phase to another is a deeply personal decision, but most people eventually want or need to dial things back seriously. Over time, you just become less obsessed with trying to be connected on the business side, and you spend more and more time on yourself. So even the rewired may finally fully retire. In terms of the business world—which is not all of life, by any means— the sequence is rewired, retired, irrelevant. But don't take this personally. By the time you become irrelevant to the business world, the business world will probably be irrelevant to you.

LESSON: No matter how you find satisfaction— continuing to work, full- or part-time, committing to something new, or simply putting your feet up—is up to you. If you're lucky enough to have choices, think them through and choose them consciously.

We do live in a very youth-oriented society, which can lead to other sorts of irrelevance when people give up the effort to keep up with changing technology or just to keep up with the world at large. Older people deserve some measure of respect for their experience and knowledge, but they shouldn't get a special dispensation when it comes to adding value. The older people we enjoy are those who make the effort to stay young in spirit and remain open to the world.

Looking back over our careers and what advice we might offer our younger selves, Ilene would tell herself not to worry so much about reaching her destination. She used to always fret about her career— would she ever be a CEO? This always involves some element of luck. Was she in the right time and place? That's difficult to gauge until you're well along the path. But beginning in consulting, back when it was more like working in a startup than in an established industry, turned out to be a good move. Moving to the corporate world was another good move for her, one that suited her temperament and skills. She would tell her younger self, "Relax! One way or another, you'll get there."

Bram, meanwhile, is more focused on the journey rather than the destination. Life is full of peaks and valleys, and he would urge his younger self to savor the peaks, to fully enjoy the good moments for all they're worth. Not that he hasn't enjoyed life, but there's always room for improvement—just as with a golf swing. There's a saying in golf—he swung within himself, meaning it was smooth, it was balanced. Bram feels he lived the peaks within himself.

LESSON: When you're younger, try to relax and enjoy both your career and your life. Savor the high points and be confident that you will find your path. As you reach the latter stages of your career, take time to plan your rewiring. Then, enjoy this next phase of life, with more time and more freedom than you've had before.

Acknowledgments

It is our belief that dual-career couples are key to creating a better and more equitable world. And we also believe that dual-career couples don't yet get all the recognition, understanding and support they need. This is the reason we wrote this book. It would not have been possible without people who shared our vision about the relevance of dual-career couples. More importantly, this book could never have been written if it weren't for all of those who made it possible for us to succeed as a dual-career couple with a family.

Seth Green, dean of the Graham School of Continuing Liberal and Professional Studies at the University of Chicago, was among the first advocates for this book. When we were still nurturing the idea of promoting dual-career couples, Seth invited us to speak at the Baumhart Center for Social Enterprise & Responsibility at Loyola University Chicago. As the founder of the Baumhart Center, Seth approaches business and management as integral parts of a broader set of social values, including family. He saw right away that the ability for spouses to equitably pursue their career goals while also being a happy family is often missing in our society, and that our successes can serve as an example for others. He helped us hone some of the early messaging of the book, and was kind enough to review the final manuscript, even though he was in the middle of a major career move at the time.

Our friends (and former colleagues of Bram at A.T. Kearney) David Hanfland, Partner and Head of Americas at Kearney, and Beth Bovis, Partner at Kearney, also took the time and effort to review the manuscript, providing detailed and thoughtful comments.

We would also like to thank the following organizations, which have invited us to speak at meetings and webinars, including Columbia Business School, MIT Sloan, University of Miami Business School, Wharton Alumni of Los Angeles and *The Wall Street Journal*.

The many messages and questions that we received following our presentations reinforced our belief about the need for this book. Young professionals emailed us wondering how and when to approach their organizations about equitable treatment of dual-career couples and how to split household chores with their spouses. Meanwhile, students wanted to know about dating the right person, choosing the right careers and making it as a woman in the business world. We thank you for your interest and encouragement and hope that our book answers at least some of your questions.

We also appreciate Dan Bigman, editor in chief at the Chief Executive Group. Dan heard about our success in telling our story to over 500 MBA students and alumni and encouraged us to commit our experience to paper. He also introduced us to Kasia and Hugo Moreno, who helped us bring our voice to our story as an article.

Then came the time to write the book. Kasia and Hugo Moreno helped us further refine our message and make it clear! As longtime writers and editors at financial magazines such as *Forbes* and WSJ's *SmartMoney*, and as book authors, they had just the right kind of writing chops and knowledge of the business world that we were looking for. As a dual-career couple with a family themselves, they understood the potential pitfalls of being a working couple, but also knew that it was possible to make it work. And while we thought we had our story all fleshed out, they kept asking questions, uncovering new angles and going deeper into areas that we had not previously considered. This book reflects our story and our voice, written in their prose.

Our professional careers are a big part of our lives and our book, and along the way we had the support and mentorship of bosses and colleagues who helped us succeed. They helped not only with the professional aspects, but also with balancing work and family. We salute other professional dual-career couples with whom we have worked, including Cuneyt and Margo Oge, and Scott and Donna Williamson (who shared an apartment with Ilene at MIT Sloan and spent time on an interview for this book)—we learned together to cope with the challenges of balancing marriage and children with a big career.

Monte Haymon, Ilene's boss and mentor at Packaging Corp of America (a unit of Tenneco) throughout the 1980s, was an early supporter of women in the workplace. Monte helped Ilene understand the profit and loss equation of a business and the importance of key metrics. He was a numbers person with a soul. While the two of them were visiting a plant in Milwaukee, Ilene climbed on top of a table to speak to the employees, with Monte's approval. The experience taught her about interacting and communicating directly with employees. (However, she chose to "manage by walking around" and talking to people once she became CEO, not habitually climb tables.) As a father of three daughters, Monte also made sure that work wouldn't get in the way of Ilene's being a mom. On Halloween, he told her to not hold any meetings after 4pm and go trick-or-treating with her kids.

Dana Mead, CEO of Tenneco throughout most of the 1990s, was Ilene's boss when she was the company's vice president of operations. He mentored her about leadership. A former military and West Point guy, Dana took the whole executive team to Gettysburg, where they walked the field all day and discussed the battle. Dana believed in setting big goals and leading from the front. He involved Ilene in setting up a Center for Creative Leadership program for Tenneco. And while he never explicitly talked about family, he made it possible for Ilene to balance family and work. He did not insist that she move to Houston, where the company was based, but encouraged her to participate in weekly meetings, either in person or by phone from Chicago.

Ilene also would like to recognize the collaborative teamwork of her colleagues on the executive teams at Tenneco, Alcan and Corn Products/Ingredion, and fellow board members on the boards of AJ Gallagher, United Stationers, Corn Products/Ingredion, International Paper and Lockheed Martin. Her French colleagues at Pechiney showed Ilene how to run a global company across multiple time zones, while at the same time recognizing that family is the top priority.

Bram is grateful to his team at A.T. Kearney in Detroit for creating the atmosphere of a home away from home and for inspiring him to be the best that he could be at his job. Without their support he could not have accomplished as much as he did during his time commuting between Chicago and Detroit for 10 years. They were understanding of his running back and forth between the cities and constantly multitasking. On the evenings he spent in Detroit they socialized as a family of professionals. Back home in Chicago, Joe Raudabaugh, Justin Zubrod, Laura Sue D'Annunzio and, in New York, Scott Corwin were invaluable partners, always helping him to focus on the most important issues and to let go of the small stuff.

Bram has always thanked his colleagues at The Boston Consulting Group for helping him learn to be a good consultant. He is also grateful to his partners at Booz Allen Hamilton, who taught him to be a good partner. Cyrus Freidheim gave Bram the chance to be a partner, and he and Mitzi always encouraged both Ilene and Bram at every opportunity. And he's grateful to his colleagues at A.T. Kearney, where he learned how to build an account, a practice and a firm.

Bram would also like to thank all of his clients over the years—first, for accepting his advice, and, second, for accommodating his schedule when he asked to change the time of a meeting to benefit his family. For his clients, it was a minor ask to adjust the schedule, but for Bram it made a huge difference. Bram hopes that more bosses and clients realize that a simple small act of kindness in business life can have cascading impacts when helping others maintain their own work-life balance. This will make for happier employees and better business.

Fred Wackerle and Barbara Provus, both executive recruiters, have been our mentors and supporters. While we first met on a professional basis, the relationship soon evolved into a lifelong friendship. We are grateful for the sage advice about our careers they gave us as well as the great conversation over Friday dinners and games of golf. As executive recruiters who have dealt with other peoples' careers and life-balance issues, Fred and Barbara understood the need for our book and encouraged us to write it.

On the home front, Cindy Gamboa held the fort for 16 years as our children's live-in nanny. She deserves much of the credit for our being able to become a dual-career couple with a family. She created stability and calm at home and gave us peace of mind, so that we were able to navigate corporate challenges and accomplish our professional goals without constantly worrying if the kids were okay. She gave our kids the structure they needed: Monday night was potato night, Tuesday was pizza night. She taught them to love Filipino food. When he left home, Andrew got his own rice cooker—like the one that Cindy used in our house—to make Filipino food. As Andrew and Emily became teenagers, Cindy acted as the adult supervisor for them and their friends and, in spite of her gentle manner, won their respect.

Cindy was very nurturing, and she was and remains a very special person to our children till today, having become part of our extended family. We continue to stay in touch, and Emily is also still friends with the Filipino friends she made through Cindy. We realize that many parents, especially mothers, may be wary of the special bond their children have with their babysitters. That was never the case with Cindy and us. She never tried to take our place but made sure the kids knew that we were the parents, and that we loved them even if we didn't spend every moment with them. We thought that, in our absence, she was the best person to be with our kids.

Our parents and siblings have been supportive of our choices, even though it meant that we could not see each other as much as they might have wanted to. They recognized that we had chosen our own path and let us pursue it guilt-free.

Throughout our lives, we have remained close with our siblings, and now that we are rewired, we are closer to them than ever. They have always been the proverbial older brothers and sisters (Ilene's younger brother died young), ready to give us advice and encouragement when needed and assure us that things will be all right. We admire how wisely they have chosen to live their lives, and appreciate all their respective achievements. Without them, we would not have been able to turn out the way we have.

The two most important people in our lives, who made us a family—Emily and Andrew—are the most wonderful human beings we could imagine as our children. They have been with us on this journey from day one, having embraced—without any fuss—growing up with a mother and a father both of whom worked outside the home. Even when they fully realized that, in that sense, we were different from many of their friends' parents, they never complained. They chose to make the most of every moment we had together with them rather than sulk about the time we spent apart.

We may have not always been in proximity as a family but, emotionally speaking, we were there for one another always. Today, we both work with our kids (especially Bram) and spend a lot of time together with Emily and Andrew and his family. We are grateful that they both remained in Chicago, which makes staying in touch that much easier. Being able to live close to our grandchildren makes us appreciate even more the greatest gift that our parents gave us—the chance to chart our own path and live it.

Our children are reaching the age of 40, and are now completely independent adults, following their own paths. While we are always here for them, we understand that they are living their own lives and we know that, owing to the kind of people they have chosen to be, they will continue to live wisely. We are grateful that they have made our lives full.

About the Authors

Ilene Gordon

As former CEO and chairman of Ingredion, a Fortune 500 food ingredient manufacturer, Ilene's career was defined by breaking barriers and transforming the food industry for the better. She was responsible for leading the company from $3.9 billion to nearly $6 billion in sales from 2009 to 2017. Previously, she was president and CEO of Alcan Packaging, a $6.5 billion global packaging business based in Paris, France. Ilene spent the first 17 years of her corporate career in executive roles of increasing responsibility at the Packaging Corporation of America, a division of Tenneco Inc., and at Signode, a leading global packaging company specializing in materials handling. She started her working life at the Boston Consulting Group (BCG) as a strategy consultant based in the Boston, London and Chicago offices. Currently, Ilene is presiding director of International Paper, a director of Lockheed Martin, and on the public board of IFF (International Flavors and Fragrances). Ilene is also a board member as a past chairman of the board of The Economic Club of Chicago and on the executive board Americas of MIT Sloan. She also sits on the investment committees for her daughter's and son's firms, BEA Real Estate and Bluestein Ventures. Ilene holds a B.S in mathematics, Phi Beta Kappa, from the Massachusetts Institute of Technology (MIT) in Cambridge, Mass., and an M.S. in management from MIT's Sloan School of Management.

Bram Bluestein

Bram had a successful 40-year career as a management consultant, helping companies across many industries transform their businesses. As a senior partner at A.T. Kearney, Bram led the global industry practices for Kearney and EDS Solutions Consulting and developed the textbook on account management while leading the firm's largest account team. As a senior partner at Booz Allen, Bram led the global automotive practice and advised clients in the U.S. and around the world. He started his consulting career at the Boston Consulting Group, working in the Boston, Johannesburg, London and Chicago offices. After his consulting years, Bram was involved in building McNally Capital, enabling family offices to capitalize on opportunities in the private equity space. He then cofounded, with his son Andrew, Bluestein Ventures, a venture capital firm investing in the future of food. He is also an advisor to his daughter's real-estate and property-management firm, BEA Real Estate. Bram received a B.S. in Chemistry from Lafayette College and holds an MBA from the Columbia University Graduate School of Business. Prior to starting his consulting career, Bram served in the U.S. Army and worked at the Federal Trade Commission.

Ilene and Bram have been happily married for more than 40 years and have a daughter and a son. They divide their time mainly between Chicago and Fort Lauderdale.

Endnotes

INTRODUCTION

[1] "Employment Characteristics of Families—2019," Bureau of Labor Statistics, April 2020
https://www.bls.gov/news.release/archives/famee_04212020.htm

[2] https://haas.berkeley.edu/equity/industry/playbooks/supporting-dual-career-couples/

[3] Ibid.

[4] Nancy Colier LCSW, "Can a Relationship Recover from Resentment?" *Psychology Today*, November 21, 2017
https://www.psychologytoday.com/us/blog/inviting-monkey-tea/201711/can-relationship-recover-resentment

[5] Andrea Ovans, "How Emotional Intelligence Became a Key Leadership Skill," *Harvard Business Review*, April 28, 2015
https://hbr.org/2015/04/how-emotional-intelligence-became-a-key-leadership-skill

CHAPTER 1: BEING THE RIGHT PARTNER

[6] Helen Gurley Brown, *Sex and the Single Girl*, Barricade Books (reprint edition) 2003

[7] Press release, Monster Workplace Dating Poll, February 11, 2014
https://www.businesswire.com/news/home/20140211005135/en/Keeping-it-Professional-Global-Poll-Finds-58-Think-an-Office-Romance-Would-Harm-Their-Career

[8] Press release, CareerBuilder's Annual Valentine's Day Survey, February 1, 2018
http://press.careerbuilder.com/2018-02-01-Office-Romance-Hits-10-Year-Low-According-to-CareerBuilders-Annual-Valentines-Day-Survey

[9] Rosenfeld et al., "Disintermediating your friends: How online dating in the United States displaces other ways of meeting," Proceedings of the National Academy of Sciences of the Unites States of America, 2019
https://www.pnas.org/content/116/36/17753

[10] David Masci, "Shared religious beliefs in marriage important to some, but not all, married Americans," Pew Research Center, October 27, 2016
https://www.pewresearch.org/fact-tank/2016/10/27/shared-religious-beliefs-in-marriage-important-to-some-but-not-all-married-americans/

[11] "How Fathers Influence Their Daughters' Careers," *Forbes.com*, June 14, 2010
https://www.forbes.com/2010/06/14/fathers-daughters-career-forbes-woman-leadership-success/?sh=5e7de1004dce

[12] Lauren Vinopal, "How Fathers of Daughters Can Help Women Make More Money," yahoo!news, July 15, 2019
https://news.yahoo.com/fathers-daughters-help-women-more-203122977.html

[13] Linda Nielsen, "Young Adult Daughters' Relationships With Their Fathers: Review of Recent Research," *Marriage and Family Review*, April 2014
https://www.researchgate.net/publication/271749756_Young_Adult_Daughters%27_Relationships_With_Their_Fathers_Review_of_Recent_Research

[14] Dina Gerdeman, "Kids of Working Moms Grow into Happy Adults," Working Knowledge, Harvard Business School, July 16, 2018
https://hbswk.hbs.edu/item/kids-of-working-moms-grow-into-happy-adults

[15] Michael Noer, "Don't Marry Career Women," *Forbes.com*, April 22, 2006
https://www.forbes.com/2006/08/21/careers-marriage-dating_cx_mn_0821women/?sh=6e6fdec715c7

[16] "Women in the labor force: a databook," *BLS Reports*, December 2019
https://www.bls.gov/opub/reports/womens-databook/2019/home.htm

[17] "Women in the labor force: a databook," *BLS Reports*, December 2015
www.bls.gov › opub › archive › women-in-the-labor-force-a-databook-2015

[18] The Rise in Dual Income Couples, Pew Research Center, June 18, 2015
https://www.pewresearch.org/ft_dual-income-households-1960-2012-2/

[19] Jennifer Petriglieri, "How Dual-Career Couples Make It Work," *Harvard Business Review*, September-October 2019
https://hbr.org/2019/09/how-dual-career-couples-make-it-work

[20] Shauna H. Springer, Ph.D., "Key Factors That Impact Your Odds of Marital Success," *Psychology Today*, June 30, 2012
https://www.psychologytoday.com/au/blog/the-joint-adventures-well-educated-couples/201206/key-factors-impact-your-odds-marital-success

[21] "Factors in a Successful Marriage," Divorce Source, May 16, 2016
https://www.divorcesource.com/blog/factors-in-a-successful-marriage/

CHAPTER 2: FINDING THE RIGHT CITY

[22] Numbeo, "America: Current Cost of Living by City"
https://www.numbeo.com/cost-of-living/region_rankings_current.jsp?region=019

[23] "The future of work in America," McKinsey Global Institute, 2019
https://www.mckinsey.com/featured-insights/future-of-work/the-future-of-work-in-america-people-and-places-today-and-tomorrow

[24] Quality of living city ranking, Mercer, 2019
https://mobilityexchange.mercer.com/insights/quality-of-living-rankings

[25] Annie Pilon, "This Mid Atlantic City is Tops for Women-Owned Businesses in the U.S.," *Small Business Trends*, March 2018
https://smallbiztrends.com/2017/10/top-city-for-women-owned-businesses.html

[26] Family Today, A Study of U.S. Families, conducted by Lake Research Partners for AARP, September 2012
https://www.aarp.org/content/dam/aarp/research/surveys_statistics/general/2012/
Family-Today-A-Study-of-US-Families-AARP.pdf

[27] Study.eu, "The academic backgrounds of the world's most powerful CEOs," December 19, 2017
https://www.study.eu/article/the-academic-backgrounds-of-the-worlds-most-powerful-ceos

[28] Maddux, William and Galinsky, Adam, "Cultural borders and mental barriers: The relationship between living abroad and creativity," *Journal of Personality and Social Psychology*, Vol 96(5), May 2009, 1047-1061
https://www.semanticscholar.org/paper/Cultural-borders-and-mental-barriers%3A-the-between-Maddux-Galinsky/23376f80a4a1ed7c002c7fdfc84a47d1d6d6af98

[29] Hajo Adam et al., "How Living Abroad Helps You Develop a Clearer Sense of Self," *Harvard Business Review*, May 22, 2018
https://hbr.org/2018/05/how-living-abroad-helps-you-develop-a-clearer-sense-of-self

[30] Kim Hart, "The new relocation test: Jobs for spouses," *Axios*, December 31, 2019
https://www.axios.com/jobs-spouses-dual-career-households-relocate-b9ab1eb2-f25b-4a5c-896f-c6923daf134d.html

[31] Danielle Lindemann, *Commuter Spouses: New Families in a Changing World,* ILR Press, March 15, 2019

[32] Megan Bearce, *Super Commuter Couples,* Equanimity Press, October 22, 2013

CHAPTER 3: FORGING SEPARATE PROFESSIONAL IDENTITIES AT WORK, BUT ONE AT HOME

[33] Elizabeth Aura McClintock, "Should Marriage Still Involve Changing a Woman's Name?" *Psychology Today*, September 6, 2018
https://www.psychologytoday.com/us/blog/it-s-man-s-and-woman-s-world/201809/should-marriage-still-involve-changing-womans-name

[34] Kopelman et al., "The Bride Is Keeping Her Name: A 35-Year Analysis of Trends and Correlates," *Social Behavior and Personality,* June 2009
https://www.researchgate.net/publication/233704592_The_Bride_is_Keeping__her_Name_A_35-Year_Retrospective_Analysis_of_Trends_and_Correlates

[35] Chloe Angyall, "More Women Are Taking Their Husbands' Last Names—Sort Of," *The Cut*, February 11, 2013
https://www.thecut.com/2013/02/more-women-are-taking-husbands-names-sort-of.html

[36] Dorie Clark, "How to Change Your Name and Keep Your Professional Identity," *Harvard Business Review*, December 9, 2014
https://hbr.org/2014/12/how-to-change-your-name-and-keep-your-professional-identity

[37] Kopelman et al., "The Bride Is Keeping Her Name," *Social Behavior and Personality,* June 2009
https://www.researchgate.net/publication/233704592_The_Bride_is_Keeping_her_Name_A_35-Year_Retrospective_Analysis_of_Trends_and_Correlates

[38] Elizabeth Bernstein, "When You Can't Stop Competing With Your Spouse," *Wall Street Journal,* July 30, 2018
https://www.wsj.com/articles/when-you-cant-stop-competing-with-your-spouse-1532956525

[39] Abraham Tesser, "Self-esteem maintenance in family dynamics," *Journal of Personality and Social Psychology*, 1980
https://psycnet.apa.org/record/1981-23549-001

[40] Claire Cain Miller, "Women Did Everything Right. Then Work Got 'Greedy.' *New York Times,* April 26, 2019
https://www.nytimes.com/2019/04/26/upshot/women-long-hours-greedy-professions.html

[41] Botelho et al., "The Fastest Path to the CEO Job, According to a 10-Year Study," *Harvard Business Review,* January 31, 2018
https://hbr.org/2018/01/the-fastest-path-to-the-ceo-job-according-to-a-10-year-study

CHAPTER 4: BUILDING YOUR FAMILY BECOMES YOUR PRIORITY

[42] Statista Research Department, "Average number of own children under 18 in families with children in the United States from 1960 to 2020," Statista, December 2020
https://www.statista.com/statistics/718084/average-number-of-own-children-per-family/

[43] Sharon E. Kirmeyer, Ph.D., and Brady E. Hamilton, Ph.D., "Childbearing Differences Among Three Generations of U.S. Women," Centers for Disease Control and Prevention, *NCHS Data Brief* No. 68, August 2011
https://www.cdc.gov/nchs/products/databriefs/db68.htm

[44] Cohn, Livingston and Wang, "After Decades of Decline, a Rise in Stay-at-Home Mothers," Pew Research, April 8, 2014
https://www.pewresearch.org/social-trends/2014/04/08/after-decades-of-decline-a-rise-in-stay-at-home-mothers/

[45] Sheryl Sandberg, *Lean In: Women, Work, and the Will to Lead,* Knopf, 2013

[46] Marianne Bertrand, "The Glass Ceiling," Coase Lecture, London School of Economics, 2017
https://onlinelibrary.wiley.com/doi/abs/10.1111/ecca.12264

[47] Robert D. Mare, "Educational Homogamy in Two Gilded Ages: Evidence from Inter-generational Social Mobility Data," *Annals of the American Academy of Political and Social Science,* December 10, 2015
https://journals.sagepub.com/doi/abs/10.1177/0002716215596967

[48] Hana Schank and Elizabeth Wallace, "How Much Ambition Can a Marriage Sustain?" *The Atlantic,* December 19, 2016
https://www.theatlantic.com/business/archive/2016/12/conservation-of-ambition/507980/

[49] Cohn, Livingston and Wang, "After Decades of Decline, a Rise in Stay-at-Home Mothers," Pew Research, April 8, 2014
https://www.pewresearch.org/social-trends/2014/04/08/after-decades-of-decline-a-rise-in-stay-at-home-mothers/

[50] Ibid.

[51] Marguerite Ward and Rachel Gillett, "Science says parents of successful kids have these 24 things in common," *businessinsider.com,* September 2, 2020
https://www.businessinsider.com/how-parents-set-their-kids-up-for-success-2016-4

[52] Wendy Klein, Carolina Izquierdo and Thomas N. Bradbury, "The Difference Between a Happy Marriage and a Miserable One: Chores," *The Atlantic,* March 1, 2013
https://www.theatlantic.com/sexes/archive/2013/03/the-difference-between-a-happy-marriage-and-miserable-one-chores/273615/

[53] Press release, Bright Horizons, "Modern Family Index Shows Motherhood Penalty in American Workplace," January 28, 2019
https://www.brighthorizons.com/newsroom/modern-family-index-2018

[54] Ibid.

[55] Modern Marriage, Pew Research Center, 2007
https://www.pewresearch.org/social-trends/2007/07/18/modern-marriage/

[56] Duckworth et al., "Grit: Perseverance and passion for long-term goals," *Journal of Personality and Social Psychology*, 2016
https://www.researchgate.net/publication/6290064_Grit_Perseverance_and_P assion_for_Long-Term_Goals

CHAPTER 5: WALKING THE TIGHTROPE OF WORK-LIFE BALANCE

[57] Dianne Grande, "Date Night: Not a Luxury, a Necessity," *Psychology Today*, March 30, 2017
https://www.psychologytoday.com/us/blog/in-it-together/201703/date-night-not-luxury-necessity

[58] Press release, University of Minnesota, "Make Time for Your Spouse—Couples That Spend Time Together Are Happier Individuals," February 10, 2016
https://twin-cities.umn.edu/news-events/make-time-your-spouse-couples-spend-time-together-are-happier-individuals

[59] Sanjay Salomon, "Study: Employers, Employees Don't Agree on Work-Life Balance," *Boston.com*, February 4, 2015
https://www.boston.com/news/jobs/2015/02/04/study-employers-employees-dont-agree-on-work-life-balance/

[60] *Global generations: A global study on work-life challenges across generations*, EY 2015
http://cs-wordpress.s3.amazonaws.com › 2015/06

[61] Bergman, P., "How (and why) to stop multitasking," *Harvard Business Review*, May 20, 2010
https://hbr.org/2010/05/how-and-why-to-stop-multitaski

[62] "The Myth of Multitasking," *Scientific American*, July 2009
https://www.scientificamerican.com/podcast/episode/the-myth-of-multitasking-09-07-15/

[63] John Medina, *Brain Rules*, Pear Press, 2014

[64] "Business Travel by the Numbers," Trondent Development Corp.
https://www.trondent.com/business-travel-statistics/

[65] "105 Critical Business Travel Statistics: 2021/2022 Spending & Concerns Analysis," financesonline.com
https://financesonline.com/business-travel-statistics

[66] Chris McGinnis, "Top jobs that involve heavy travel," BBC, November 11, 2011

https://www.bbc.com/travel/article/20111111-top-jobs-that-involve-heavy-business-travel?OCID=fbtvl

CHAPTER 6: MANAGING MONEY

[67] Jeff Schmidt, "Consulting Pay: What Undergrads and MBAs Earned in 2019," *Poets & Quants for Undergrads,* January 21, 2020

https://poetsandquantsforundergrads.com/2020/01/21/consulting-pay-what-undergrads-and-mbas-earned-in-2019/

[68] Katie Brockman, "This Is How Much the Average American Household Saves Each Year," The Motley Fool, October 27, 2019

https://www.fool.com/retirement/2019/10/27/this-is-how-much-the-average-american-saves-each-y.aspx

[69] Jessica Dickler, "75 percent of Americans are winging it when it comes to their financial future," CNBC.com, April 2, 2019

https://www.cnbc.com/2019/04/01/when-it-comes-to-their-financial-future-most-americans-are-winging-it.html

CHAPTER 7: MAKING TRADEOFFS

[70] Eric Suni, "How Much Sleep Do We Really Need?" National Sleep Foundation, March 20, 2021

https://www.sleepfoundation.org/how-sleep-works/how-much-sleep-do-we-really-need

[71] Elizabeth Mendes, Lydia Saad and Kyley McGeeney, "Stay-at-Home Moms Report More Depression, Sadness, Anger, Gallup, May 18, 2012

https://news.gallup.com/poll/154685/stay-home-moms-report-depression-sadness-anger.aspx

[72] Emilia Bunea, Svetlana N. Khapova and Evgenia I. Lysova, "Why CEOs Devote So Much Time to Their Hobbies," *Harvard Business Review,* October 8, 2018

https://hbr.org/2018/10/why-ceos-devote-so-much-time-to-their-hobbies

[73] Michael E. Porter and Nitin Nohria, "How CEOs Manage Time," *Harvard Business Review,* July-August 2018

https://hbr.org/2018/07/how-ceos-manage-time

[74] Bunea, et al., "Why CEOs Devote So Much Time to Their Hobbies," *Harvard Business Review,* October 8, 2018

https://hbr.org/2018/10/why-ceos-devote-so-much-time-to-their-hobbies

CHAPTER 8: EMBRACING TECHNOLOGY

75 Social Media Today, March 23, 2019
https://www.socialmediatoday.com/

76 Hardik Shah, "App Usage Statistics 2021 that'll Surprise You (Updated)," January 5, 2021
https://www.simform.com/the-state-of-mobile-app-usage/

77 "Motorola DynaTAC," *Wikipedia*
https://en.wikipedia.org/wiki/Motorola_DynaTAC

78 Sharita Forrest, University of Illinois at Urbana–Champaign, "Study: Families spend half of their evening meal distracted by technology, tasks," *MedicalXpress*, April 2019
https://medicalxpress.com/news/2019-04-families-evening-meal-distracted-technology.html

79 "Americans Don't Want to Unplug from Phones While on Vacation, Despite Latest Digital Detox Trend," Asurion press release, May 17, 2018
https://www.asurion.com/about/press-releases/americans-dont-want-to-unplug-from-phones-while-on-vacation-despite-latest-digital-detox-trend/

80 "The @Work State of Mind," *Forbes* and Gyro, 2012
https://www.forbes.com/forbesinsights/atwork_state_of_mind/

81 Kasia Moreno, "When Is It Okay To Send Weekend Work Emails?" *Forbes*, 2012
https://www.forbes.com/sites/forbesinsights/2012/04/24/when-is-it-okay-to-send-weekend-work-emails/?sh=5c53a7b04677

82 Economic news release, "Time adults spent caring for children as a primary activity, by age of youngest child, averages for May to December, 2019 and 2020," U.S. Bureau of Labor Statistics
https://www.bls.gov/news.release/atus.t06.htm

83 Zara Abrams, "The Future of Remote Work," *Monitor on Psychology*, Vol. 50, No. 9, American Psychological Association, October 1, 2019
https://www.apa.org/monitor/2019/10/cover-remote-work

84 Dana Wilkie, "Will Remote Work Hinder Careers?," SHRM, June 2020

https://www.shrm.org/resourcesandtools/hr-topics/people-managers/pages/coronavirus-career-progression-.aspx

[85] Elissa Liu, "How Many Fortune 500 CEOs Are on Social Media?" *influentialexecutive.com*, August 8, 2020
https://influentialexecutive.com/how-many-fortune-500-ceos-social-media-2020/

[86] The Company Behind the Brand: In Reputation We Trust," Weber Shandwick and KRC Research, 2012
https://www.webershandwick.com/news/the-company-behind-the-brand-the-indivisibility-of-the-company-and-product/

[87] Tom Peters, "The Brand Called You," *FastCompany*, August 31, 1997
https://www.fastcompany.com/28905/brand-called-you

[88] Moss Clement, "4 Effective Ways to Use Technology to Improve Work-Life Balance," *greycampus.com*, May 7, 2020
https://www.greycampus.com/blog/others/effective-ways-to-use-technology-to-improve-work-life-balance

CHAPTER 9: WEATHERING THE COVID STRESS TEST—THE HYBRID WORKPACE AND THE POST-PANDEMIC AFTERMATH

[89] Lauren Weber, Vanessa Fuhrmans, "How the Coronavirus Crisis Threatens to Set Back Women's Careers, *The Wall Street Journal*, September 2020
https://www.wsj.com/articles/how-the-coronavirus-crisis-threatens-to-set-back-womens-careers-11601438460

[90] "Women in the Workplace 2020," by McKinsey and LeanIn.org
https://www.mckinsey.com/featured-insights/diversity-and-inclusion/women-in-the-workplace

[91] Feng, Z. and Savani, K. (2020), "Covid-19 created a gender gap in perceived work productivity and job satisfaction: implications for dual-career parents working from home," *Gender in Management*, Vol. 35 No. 7/8, pp. 719-736
https://www.researchgate.net/publication/344643089_Covid-19_created_a_gender_gap_in_perceived_work_productivity_and_job_satisfaction_implications_for_dual-career_parents_working_from_home

[92] Jennifer Petriglieri, "How Dual-Career Couples Can Work Through the Coronavirus Crisis," *Harvard Business Review*, March 2020
https://hbr.org/2020/03/how-dual-career-couples-can-work-through-the-coronavirus-crisis

[93] Shockley et al., "Work-Family Strategies during COVID-19: Examining Gender Dynamics among Dual-Earner Couples with Young Children," *Journal of Applied Psychology*, November 5, 2020
https://www.researchgate.net/publication/346648969_Work-family_strategies_during_COVID-19_Examining_gender_dynamics_among_dual-earner_couples_with_young_children

[94] Tariro Mzezewa, "The Flight Goes Nowhere. And It's Sold Out." *New York Times*, September 19, 2020
https://www.nytimes.com/2020/09/19/travel/airlines-pandemic-flights-to-nowhere.html

[95] Kasia Moreno, "Silver Linings: Key Lessons From How We Communicate In The New Normal," *Forbes*, November 2020
https://www.forbes.com/sites/insights-zoom/2020/11/20/silver-linings-key-lessons-from-how-we-communicate-in-the-new-normal/?sh=3e8ed9292784

[96] McKinsey Global Institute, "The future of work after COVID-19," February 2021
https://www.mckinsey.com/featured-insights/future-of-work/the-future-of-work-after-covid-19

[97] McKinsey Corporate Business Functions Practice, "Reimagine: Preparing for SG&A in the next normal," McKinsey.com, November 2020
https://www.mckinsey.com/business-functions/operations/our-insights/reimagine-preparing-for-sga-in-the-next-normal

[98] Brooke Alloco, Deborah Lovich and Michelle Stohlmeyer Russell, "Making the Workplace Work for Dual-Career Couples," BCG.com, July 25, 2018
https://www.bcg.com/publications/2018/making-workplace-work-dual-career-couples

[99] Andrew Pham, "Supporting Dual Career Couples in the Age of Covid-19," Center for Equity, Gender, and Leadership, UC Berkeley, July 15, 2020
https://berkeleyequity.medium.com/supporting-dual-career-couples-in-the-age-of-covid-19-49d2763b7ed0

[100] Anisa Purbasari Horton, "Why it's so hard for you and your partner to both have successful careers," *FastCompany*, September 26, 2019
https://www.fastcompany.com/90407484/company-policies-can-help-dual-career-couples-make-it-work

[101] Nellie Bowles, "They Can't Leave the Bay Area Fast Enough," *New York Times,* January 17, 2021
https://www.nytimes.com/2021/01/14/technology/san-francisco-covid-work-moving.html

[102] United States Industrial Outlook, JLL
https://www.us.jll.com/en/trends-and-insights/research/industrial-market-statistics-trends

[103] "Hi, remote wortkers!" Tulsa Remote
tulsaremote.org

[104] McKinsey Global Institute, "The future of work after COVID-19," February 2021
https://www.mckinsey.com/featured-insights/future-of-work/the-future-of-work-after-covid-19

[105] Ibid.

[106] Ibid.

[107] Scott McCartney, "The Covid pandemic could cut business travel by 36 percent—permanently," *The Wall Street Journal,* December 1, 2020
https://www.wsj.com/articles/the-covid-pandemic-could-cut-business-travel-by-36permanently-11606830490

CHAPTER 10: "REWIRING"—NOT RETIRING

[108] John Elflein, "Life expectancy – Men at the age of 65 years in the U.S. 1960-2018," October 15, 2020
https://www.statista.com/statistics/266657/us-life-expectancy-for-men-aat-the-age-of-65-years-since-1960/

[109] "Labor force projections to 2024: The labor force is growing, but slowly," Monthly Labor Review, U.S. Bureau of Labor Statistics, December 2015
https://www.bls.gov/opub/mlr/2015/article/labor-force-projections-to-2024.htm

[110] "Labor force participation rate for workers age 75 and older projected to be over 10 percent by 2026," TED: The Economics Daily, U.S. Bureau of Labor Statistics, May 29, 2019
https://www.bls.gov/opub/ted/2019/labor-force-participation-rate-for-workers-age-75-and-older-projected-to-be-over-10-percent-by-2026.htm

[111] Mark Miller, "Take This Job and Love It!" *AARP The Magazine*, February/March 2015

[112] Staying Ahead of the Curve 2013: The Work and Career Study, AARP
https://www.aarp.org › research › general › 2014

[113] Mark R. Luborsky and Ian M. Leblanc, "Cross-cultural perspectives on the concept of retirement: An analytic redefinition," *Journal of Cross Cultural Gerontology*, December 2003
https://pubmed.ncbi.nlm.nih.gov/14654730/

[114] "The Go-Go, Slow-Go, and No-Go Years: A Spending Plan for All Three Phases of Retirement," Keen Wealth Advisors, October 23, 2019
https://keenwealthadvisors.com/insights/gogo-slowgo-nogo

[115] Julia Kagan, "Phases of Retirement," *Investopedia*, February 18, 2021
https://www.investopedia.com/terms/p/phases-retirement.asp

[116] "Mandatory retirement," *Wikipedia*
https://en.wikipedia.org/wiki/Mandatory_retirement

[117] "Retirement," *Wikipedia*
https://en.wikipedia.org/wiki/Retirement

[118] "Real retirement ages around the world revealed," *lovemoney.com*, November 16, 2020
https://www.lovemoney.com/galleryextended/75682/real-retirement-ages-around-the-world-revealed?page=1

DOUBLING DOWN

Made in the USA
Coppell, TX
21 March 2023

14530554R10095